Advance Praise for *My Maril*

"Old Hollywood through the eyes of a child and a young woman. When your stepmom is Jane Wyman, stepbrother is the son of Ronald Reagan (who would later become President of the United States), and surrogate mother/big sister is Marilyn Monroe, you've got some unique memories. Terry Karger delivers."

—*New York Times*
bestselling author Richard Buskin

"Terry Karger has written a remarkable story of her times with two of the most iconic, larger-than-life figures of the twentieth century, Ronald Reagan and Marilyn Monroe. She knew them before the world did. Terry had a glimpse of their down-to-earth humanity. Previously unseen photographs of Marilyn Monroe with Terry's family reveal how comfortable Marilyn was in their presence. She didn't have to impress anyone and could just be herself. If you're looking for the real Marilyn Monroe, you won't find a dumb blonde here. That was a media misperception and not who she really was. In this book, Terry wipes away the dumb blonde myth and presents an intelligent woman in Marilyn Monroe, a shy lady who was remarkably eager to improve herself at every opportunity while at the same time teaching young Terry some important lessons in life during their fourteen-year friendship."

—Hermine Hilton, author of
The Executive Memory Guide and memory
expert for Fortune 500 Companies

TERRY KARGER

with *New York Times* bestselling author **JAY MARGOLIS**

Marilyn Monroe, Ronald Reagan, Hollywood, and Me

Foreword by **MICHAEL REAGAN**

A POST HILL PRESS BOOK
ISBN: 978-1-63758-326-5
ISBN (eBook): 978-1-63758-327-2

My Maril:
Marilyn Monroe, Ronald Reagan, Hollywood, and Me
© 2022 by Terry Karger with Jay Margolis
All Rights Reserved

Post Hill Press
New York • Nashville
posthillpress.com

Published in the United States of America
1   2   3   4   5   6   7   8   9   10

CONTENTS

FOREWORD

I FIRST BECAME AWARE of Marilyn Monroe on January 5, 1953, when I was just seven years old.

My stepfather, Fred Karger, was giving a birthday party for my mother, Jane Wyman—her thirty-sixth. It was a big Hollywood party with all their friends from the film industry. So my sister Maureen and I went to William Ruser's jewelry store on Rodeo Drive in Beverly Hills to buy a present for Mom.

Before we even entered the store, I saw what I wanted to buy. In the display window was a gleaming silver serving tray. Printed on the tray was a photo of a beautiful blonde, lying on red satin, as nude as the day she was born.

She was, of course, Marilyn Monroe.

I stood on the sidewalk, unable to take my eyes off that hair, those lips, those beautiful eyes, and…everything else.

"Maureen, wait!" I said as she was about to enter the store. "Look!"

My sister, who was four years older than I, said, "Look at what?"

I pointed to the tray in the window. "Let's get that tray for Mom."

"Michael!" she said, horrified. "We can't give that to Mom!"

"Why not? It's pretty!"

"Forget it, Michael. We're getting something else."

My big sister won out. We ended up buying a sugar bowl, and we had Ruser's gift wrap it and send it over to the house.

As we walked away from the jewelry store, I cast a longing glance over my shoulder at the silver platter in the window. The luscious blonde looked back at me from her bed of red satin. I sighed.

My biggest shock was yet to come.

That night at the party, Fred and Mom gave me the job of answering the front door and admitting the guests. I'd stand there in my little suit and I'd give my little welcome speech and direct our guests to the party.

At one point the doorbell rang and I opened the door—and my jaw nearly fell off its hinges. There, on my own front porch, stood that vision of loveliness from the jewelry store window. I could hardly believe my eyes.

It was Marilyn Monroe in the flesh—but with her clothes on.

I was in awe. I couldn't think. I could barely breathe. I forgot my little rehearsed speech.

People sometimes ask me, "Michael, when did you first know there was a God?" I tell them, "The day I opened the door and found Marilyn Monroe on my doorstep."

My stepsister Terry knew Marilyn long before she became a star. Terry's dad, Fred Karger, dated Marilyn while he was her vocal coach, when Marilyn was an unknown contract player at Columbia Pictures. Fred first brought Marilyn home to meet his family when Terry was only six.

Marilyn never had a family of her own. She never knew her dad, and her birth mother had been institutionalized when Marilyn was only seven years old. Marilyn lived in foster homes and an orphanage, and she grew up feeling unwanted. When Fred Karger introduced Marilyn to his family, Marilyn adopted Fred's family as her own. And Fred's family adopted her and gave her a new name: Maril. When she needed to escape the insanity of fame, when she needed to take off the "Marilyn Monroe" disguise and feel normal and at peace, she took refuge in her adopted family.

I met Terry on Halloween night 1952. Fred and Marilyn had ended their affair several years earlier, and Fred had been dating my mother, Jane Wyman, for a while. That night, Fred brought Terry over to our house on Beverly Glen Boulevard to go trick-or-treating with Maureen and me. I had my cowboy costume on and I was ready to ring doorbells, but Mom called us all into the den. "Before you go out," she said, "there's something I want to tell you."

We all filed into the den, including Fred and Terry. Mom turned to Maureen and me and said, "Children, Fred is going to be your new father." Then she turned to Terry and said, "Terry, I'm going to be your new mother." That was Mom's way of announcing that she and Fred were getting married.

My parents, Jane Wyman and Ronald Reagan, divorced in 1949, and I only got to see Dad every other weekend as it was. When Mom said that Fred was going to be my new parent, I was afraid that Dad wouldn't be my father anymore. That fear, of course, was unfounded.

The next day, Saturday, November 1, Maureen, Terry, and I went out to the ranch with Dad. When we got home that night, Mom was gone. I asked Carrie, our housekeeper, where Mom was. She grinned and said, "She'll be back."

Sunday morning, Carrie called Maureen, Terry, and me downstairs and told us to hold out our hands. Then she filled them with rice.

I said, "What's this for?"

Carrie said, "When your mother and Fred get here, throw this rice at them."

A few minutes later, Fred and Mom drove up and announced that they had eloped to Santa Barbara. As they entered the house, Carrie signaled us, after which Terry, Maureen, and I pelted them with rice.

Then Fred asked, "Where's the toothache medicine?"—meaning, "Where's the Scotch?"

Soon after that, Terry moved in, and she was a great stepsister. She went with Maureen and me out to Dad's ranch, and the three of us had many good times together. Mom's marriage to Fred didn't last—they were granted an interlocutory divorce decree in December 1954; their first divorce finalized in 1955. They tried marriage again in 1961 but were re-divorced in 1965.

Terry and I have remained good friends even after our parents' two divorces. In fact, because of those divorces, I still kid Terry and call her my "stepsister twice removed."

Now, here's the interesting thing about Terry. You know how some people name-drop to make themselves seem important? Not Terry. She grew up around Hollywood, so she was never impressed by glitz and glamour. The biggest names in Hollywood were nobody special, just friends of her dad.

After college, Terry became a teacher. Knowing her as I do, I'll bet no one around her knew that her father was a renowned Hollywood composer who married an Oscar-winning actress, or that Marilyn Monroe used to be her friend and babysitter.

I've told Terry for years that she should write a book about Marilyn. She'd say, "No, Maril was my friend. She was always so sweet to me, and I don't want anyone to think I'm trying to profit from knowing her."

But one day, Terry said, "Michael, I've been thinking about your advice. Maybe I should write a book about Maril. She wasn't like the Marilyn Monroe you always read about. I'd like to write a book about who Maril was behind the image. And I'd like to tell the story of how she adopted my whole family as her own."

And now she has written it. As you're about to discover, it's a fascinating book.

This is a tragic story—and a beautiful one. This is not the story of "Marilyn Monroe, Movie Star," because that Marilyn was a role she played. This is the story about Terry's Maril, a sweet soul who got lost somewhere on the road to stardom.

You may think you know Marilyn Monroe's story. But the real Marilyn was so much more than the image. She was so much more than the nude girl on red satin I saw in a jewelry store window at age seven. And she was so much more than the sensational headlines that announced her death in early August 1962.

Turn the page and peek behind the image. Meet the Marilyn Monroe the world has never known before.

Meet Terry Karger's Maril.

—Michael Reagan

Michael Reagan with his father Ronald Reagan

INTRODUCTION

I SEE YOU, MARIL—AND I can't believe it. I see you when we first met on that spring day back in 1948, so full of life as you stepped out of Daddy's car onto the driveway of our West Hollywood home...and I can't believe the phone conversation he and I found ourselves having this morning after I heard the radio news.

"Daddy, they're saying it was suicide. Maril wouldn't kill herself, would she?"

"I don't know, Terry. I really don't know."

"She sounded so happy when I spoke with her a few days ago. She couldn't wait to return to work."

If you were in trouble, Maril, why didn't you reach out to us, especially to my grandmother? You've always told Nana everything, including your fears. Did those fears finally consume you? Or did something else happen last night?

* * *

August 5, 1962, was a black day for my family. Twenty-one years old, attending the University of Southern California and residing in an apartment off campus, I was in a state of shock. Six decades later, I still don't believe Maril took her own life. Yet, having consistently rejected requests to write a book about this sweet, fragile woman—because no words of mine could do her justice—I've now changed my mind.

Few books, you see, have come close to capturing the heart of the Maril I knew. Fewer still have written about her relationship with the Kargers, stretching back to her days as an unknown twenty-one-year-old starlet under contract to Columbia Pictures. So I'm sharing my memories in the hope you'll catch a glimpse of this wounded, beautiful soul who reached for fame, caught it, and frequently sought refuge from it—before suddenly passing from this world to the next and into our memories.

Maril and my father, Fred Karger, were in a romantic relationship from early March 1948 until the spring of 1949, but their friendship never went away, and she continued to be a member of our family. Whenever she came to our house, it would be with her hair under a scarf, without lipstick or makeup, enabling her to relax and be herself.

Whereas the carefully crafted media sensation known as Marilyn Monroe made an indelible impact on our culture, the quiet, shy, mischievous Maril I knew left a deep imprint on my life. That's the woman I want you to meet: the one who, in many ways, was as innocent as a child—and who loved being around kids. We, in turn, embraced her whenever life proved to be overwhelming. And her upbeat moods were so infectious that, sometimes when my eyes are closed, I can still hear Maril's laughter.

Her life, her talent, and her spirit continue to influence the world today. In 2017, the public heard a song Maril recorded with my father in 1948 for the first time in Guillermo del Toro's motion picture *The Shape of Water*, which was nominated for thirteen Oscars (del Toro won Oscars for Best Picture and Best Director) at the 90th Academy Awards.

In late 1948, my father composed a song with producer-screenwriter Alex Gottlieb called "How Wrong Can I Be?" Gottlieb lived in the apartment above the home of my maternal grandmother, Bernice Sacks, just off the Sunset Strip. Daddy wrote the music in Bernice's kitchen and Alex wrote the lyrics. They asked Marilyn to provide the vocals for the demo record. Daddy sent the demo and sheet music to a music publisher, but the publisher never returned it. The disk and its accompanying sheet music were found in the publisher's files in 1992.

On August 16, 1995, the *New York Times* reported the discovery of the record and described its sound: "Accompanied by a piano and muted trumpet, Monroe delivers the song in a torchy, seductive style with an occasional jazzy inflection… The voice is sultry, a little off-key from time to time, and instantly recognizable. 'How Wrong Can I Be?' recorded on a 12-inch acetate disc, was never released." The label on the disk, said the *Times*, reads, "Fred Karger at the piano, Manny Klein on the trumpet, vocal by Marilyn Monroe."

Biographer Stacy Eubank wrote in her book *Holding a Good Thought for Marilyn* on page 123 about a discrepancy between the record label and the sheet music: "The music and lyrics were hand-written on three pages of Holograph Musical Manuscript paper. It is interesting that credit is given to Terry Meredith [my first and middle names] and Fred Karger on the sheet music, and not to Fred Karger and Alex Gottlieb, as indicated on the acetate disk. The sheet music had a handwritten note referring to Marilyn: Marilyn Monroe sings this beautiful song in the key of 'C.'"

After remaining hidden from the public for almost seventy years, it can now be heard by millions of people in *The Shape of Water*—and that's just one of the ways Maril continues to touch our hearts and live on in our memories.

Our Maril never left us—which is why, between these pages, you'll find not only my recollections but also those of my family members.

This is a book about a free spirit tortured by a troubled mind. About naiveté wrapped in guile. And about the beauty of mutual love and unconditional friendship.

Looking back, I don't like to think about the end. But I love to remember the beginning.

1: AN INDESTRUCTIBLE DRIVE TO SUCCEED

IT WAS A BEAUTIFUL spring day when Marilyn Monroe entered my life.

Six years old, I lived with Daddy and my grandmother, who we called Nana, at 1312 North Harper Avenue in West Hollywood. It was a large house, with a rolling front lawn, a big backyard, and a long driveway leading to the garage in the back. One day in early March 1948, I was kneeling by the freshly watered flowerbed beside that driveway, dipping my hands into a muddy puddle, when I heard my father's car stop a few yards behind me.

"Hi, sweetheart."

"Hi, Daddy."

Walking around the car, he opened the passenger door and, because of that door, I could only see a lady's shapely foot and ankle. I couldn't see her face.

"Terry, I want you to meet Marilyn."

As I jumped up, Daddy's friend shook my mucky hand while pointing at the mud castle I'd been building in the flowerbed.

"That's a pretty house."

"It's a castle."

"A pretty castle, then."

Giggling, she looked happy to have Daddy slip an arm around her waist as he guided his new twenty-one-year-old girlfriend into the house. And that's how Marilyn Monroe became a part of my family and my life.

Right from the start, we were all disarmed by Maril's sweetness and innocence. To me, she was like an angel—shy and radiant, with luminescent skin and wide blue eyes that exuded both warmth and a sort of cautiousness. Perhaps she had been hurt too many times—even as a six-year-old that was my first impression. She looked scared of meeting people.

At that time, six of us were living in my grandmother Ann Karger's large house: Nana, Daddy, Aunt Mary, her children Ben and Anne, and me. So Marilyn had quite a welcoming committee—and she was clearly charmed when Nana opened her arms and gave our guest a motherly hug along with a kiss on the cheek.

"What can I do to help?" Marilyn asked Nana while clinging to Daddy.

"Not a thing, Maril dear," came the reply. "We'll have dinner on the table in no time."

With that, Marilyn Monroe acquired a new name, one that only our family called her. And she also moved into Nana's guest room for the next three weeks. (Maril would soon move in across the street at 1309 North Harper Avenue with her drama coach, Natasha Lytess.)

Marilyn Monroe in 1948
(From the collection of Terry Karger)

Before Daddy and Maril met, she'd been a houseguest of actor John Carroll and his wife Lucille Ryman, who ran MGM's talent department. From there she'd moved into the Hollywood Studio Club, a chaperoned dormitory operated by the YWCA for young women in the movie business. Located at 1215–1233 Lodi Place in the center of Hollywood, it housed many future stars, including Maureen O'Sullivan, Donna Reed, Dorothy Malone, and Kim Novak.

According to Marilyn biographer Donald Spoto, Lucille Ryman recalled how, when "Fred drove her home after their first date, she directed him not to the Studio Club but to a grimy, flea-infested Hollywood tenement (recently abandoned by another Columbia starlet); *this*, she said gloomily, was all she could afford."[1]

Maintaining a spartan lifestyle, spending very little money on food, saving most of her funds for the weekly Studio Club rent, Maril hadn't really lived in that dismal tenement. But she made Daddy think otherwise—and seeing the awful conditions there was what prompted him to invite her to our house for a home-cooked meal. That was the day Maril first shook my muddy hand.

During the initial three weeks she stayed with us, our family fell in love with her. She helped Nana with household chores, babysat my cousins and me, and drove us on errands. Yet there was one flaw in Maril's plan: instead of giving the Studio Club notice that she was moving out, she simply stopped showing up, prompting the manager to call Columbia Pictures to find out if she was all right. When Daddy heard about this, he realized he'd been deceived.

"He said that because I lied about this, he couldn't trust me with anything," Maril would recall years later. "He didn't think I would make a good example to the children in his family. It made me feel pretty rotten."[2]

My father soon forgave Maril, and their romance ended up lasting just over a year. He genuinely cared for her, but her lie may have persuaded him that he shouldn't marry her.

The rest of us Kargers only knew Maril was sweet and kind—and that she'd never had a proper family before. So when Daddy entered her life, we accepted her as one of our own while he became her teacher, lover, and in many ways a father figure.

* * *

Frederick Maxwell Karger Jr. was a vocal coach, songwriter, composer, and arranger. On March 10, 1948, Columbia boss Harry Cohn called Daddy to inform him he'd be coaching a young actress named Marilyn Monroe who'd just been put under contract. This meant elevating her pleasant but untrained singing voice to sound more professional.

Marilyn Monroe with Fred Karger in 1948
(From the collection of Terry Karger)

After he'd been doing this for only a short time, Daddy was ordered by Harry to let him hear Maril sing...*now*.

"I'm not ready," she justifiably protested. But, as my father was quick to point out, there was no arguing with the tyrannical studio head.

"You'll be fine," he assured her. "Just relax and do your best."

She wasn't fine. Frightened and shaking while Daddy drove her to the lot near the intersection of Gower Street and Sunset Boulevard,

Maril flipped through a manila folder stuffed with Christian Science literature her Aunt Ana Lower had given her. Maybe something in there might help calm her down…until they entered Harry Cohn's cavernous office.

"I heard you were a singer," Cohn boomed, a lit cigar in his mouth. "Let's see what you can do."

The piano was near the door. Harry sat behind his desk at the far end of the room, and after Daddy gave Maril a quick word of encouragement, he played the piano intro while she put down the folder and began to sing.

"Louder!" the mogul barked, prompting Daddy and Maril to stop and start again.

Listening intently for a few bars, Harry then moved closer—inadvertently brushing the manila folder and scattering Christian Science literature all around his feet. So, picking up the papers, he placed them back in the folder—before holding it above his head once Maril had finished singing.

"Do you believe in Christian Science, Miss Monroe?"

"I do."

"That's good. Keep working with Freddie. He'll make a singer out of you."

A few days later, producer Harry Romm informed Daddy he needed a supporting actress for *Ladies of the Chorus*, a musical that would soon go into production. Daddy recommended Maril.

Both he and Columbia's head drama coach, Natasha Lytess, told Maril it could be her breakout role. And although she'd soon earn a reputation for arriving late on set (or not showing up at all), Maril was completely punctual when filming *Ladies of the Chorus*, worked hard on her acting and singing, and delivered beautiful performances of two numbers, "Anyone Can See I Love You" and "Every Baby Needs a Da-Da-Daddy."

This, she hoped, would secure the renewal of her six-month contract with Columbia. But it didn't—probably because she'd made an enemy of Harry Cohn.

Sometime in mid-1948, Harry invited Maril to join him on his yacht for a trip to Catalina. Subtlety was not his forte—the "invitation" had the tone of an order, backed by a threat. So Maril politely refused, leaving Harry red-faced and furious when she managed to avoid the casting couch and slip out of his office.

"An executive tried to get me to go out on his yacht," she'd recall years later. "When I turned him down—well, we had a battle and I was fired."[3]

Ladies of the Chorus was the first and only picture Maril made for Columbia.

Beforehand, she'd spent two years as a contract player at Twentieth Century-Fox. There, in 1946, studio exec Ben Lyon convinced her to undergo a change of name from that on her birth certificate—Norma Jeane Mortenson; she sometimes went by Norma Jeane Baker—to one starting with Marilyn, after 1920s Broadway star Marilyn Miller. She then added her mother's maiden name, Monroe. (Ironically, Marilyn Monroe would later become Marilyn Miller after marrying Pulitzer Prize–winning playwright Arthur Miller.)

By the time Marilyn signed with Columbia Pictures, she had been divorced for a year and a half from Jim Dougherty, the former merchant marine she'd married at age sixteen. Meanwhile, my father was separated from my mother, Patti Sacks Karger; their divorce would be finalized in August of '48.

Daddy was handsome, elegant, and eleven years older than Marilyn, who fell deeply, wildly in love with him. They began their affair within days of first meeting.

When Columbia dropped Maril on September 8, she was hurt and her confidence was shaken. She thought she'd performed well in *Ladies of the Chorus*, so the loss of her contract stirred up old feelings of rejection and abandonment. Initially, these stemmed from the absence of her father—Charles Stanley Gifford, a work colleague of her mom, Gladys Baker, at Consolidated Film Industries. Then, when Norma Jeane was seven years old, Gladys suffered a breakdown that sent her to a mental health facility—and made her daughter a ward of the state.

Patti and Freddie Karger in the early 1940s
(From the collection of Terry Karger)

Gladys's friend Grace McKee Goddard was subsequently appointed Norma Jeane's guardian. The two women had met at Consolidated Film Industries; later they'd both work at Columbia Pictures—Gladys as a film cutter, Grace as a librarian. Yet the child still ended up living in a variety of foster homes (including Grace and Doc Goddard's) and, from age nine to eleven, at Hollywood's Los Angeles Orphans Home.

During those years, Norma Jeane became withdrawn and acquired a stutter that afflicted her as an adult whenever she felt highly stressed or insecure. The trauma of being passed from one foster home to another convinced the young girl that no one loved or wanted her.

In a rare 1950 interview, she described the emotional scars of her childhood:

"Do you know what it means to be a 'nobody'? You have no mother or father to love and care for you... If you fall and bruise your knees, or have a nightmare and wake up terrorized in the black of night, or are frightened by imaginary ghosts or monsters, or some cruel child makes fun of your clothes and shames you in front of everybody—you have no one to go to for comfort and assurance.

"That's a pretty dreadful thing for a child. It means you're not wanted. You're completely alone... The other thing I had was my dream. This was the most important. Because I was a very insecure little girl who cherished a very big and beautiful dream—a lonely kind of dream because no one paid the slightest attention to it."

1935 print sepia photograph of Marilyn Monroe (then Norma Jeane Mortenson) (From the collection of Harvey and Elsie Giffen) (The Broadway-Hollywood/Hollywood, California)

Norma Jeane was eight years old when her acting in a skit was described by a teacher as "one of the best performances I've ever seen in this school." At that moment, Norma Jeane realized that acting before an audience could generate the attention and approval she craved.

"I remember how proud I felt," Maril would recall. "It was strange and terribly exciting to know that somebody had noticed me, somebody cared about me. I was important. For the first time in my life, I mattered. I decided then and there to become an actress when I grew up…I learned to shut myself off in a private world of my own, where it was safe …

"When I was onstage I felt like an altogether different person. All my shyness and inferiority dropped from me like a cloak to the floor…I took the part of a prince disguised as a beggar who rescued the princess and lived happily ever after. I loved every minute of it, and I was so absorbed in my role."

According to Maril, the realization she wanted to be an actress "brought meaning and joy" into her life.

At age thirteen, she went to live with Grace Goddard's aunt, Ana Atchinson Lower, and commenced the happiest, most stable time of her childhood. A devout Christian Science practitioner, Aunt Ana took Norma Jeane to her church every Sunday—and told the child that she too had once dreamed of an acting career.

"I knew there was something special about you," Ana confided. "You're the daughter I always wanted… Your desire to become an actress only makes you dearer to me."

Whenever Norma Jeane became discouraged pursuing her dream, Aunt Ana would tell her, "Don't be so pessimistic. You never can tell what might happen."

The child finally felt like she belonged to someone.

"Here, at least, was someone who wanted me, someone who to me was a very beautiful person," she'd recall. "What a rush of gratitude and love swept over me when I found myself able to confess to her my deep, secret yearning to become an actress. It was like coming out of a dungeon into lovely sunshine."[4]

**When Aunt Ana Lower was younger, she once shared
Norma Jeane's dream to become an actress**

Ana Lower transformed Norma Jeane's life. And even though the teenager had to live with the Goddards when her sixty-something aunt developed high blood pressure and a heart condition, Ana and Norma Jeane continued their mother-daughter relationship through phone calls, letters, and visits.

Norma Jeane was fifteen when Doc Goddard's company transferred him to West Virginia. Because California wouldn't allow the Goddards to take their foster child out of state, Grace could no longer act as her guardian and the girl would have to go back to the orphanage—a prospect that terrified Norma Jeane. So Grace arranged a marriage between the teen and twenty-one-year-old neighbor Jim Dougherty, who'd been driving her home from school for almost two years.

Norma Jeane had a crush on Jim, and on June 19, 1942, a little more than two weeks after she turned sixteen, they were married. Thereafter, especially when Jim went to sea as a merchant marine, Norma Jeane frequently turned to Aunt Ana for advice and emotional support.

In 1945, as an officer in the US Army's First Motion Picture Unit, Ronald Reagan directed David Conover to take photographs of women at Radioplane, including Marilyn Monroe (then Norma

Jeane Dougherty), who happened to be working there at the time right before the genesis of her career.

Then, following Norma Jeane's divorce from Jim in 1946, her change of name, and her securing of bit parts in a couple of Twentieth Century-Fox movies, Ana Lower became Marilyn Monroe's first and biggest fan.

On March 14, 1948—just four days after Maril was signed by Columbia Pictures—Ana died at age sixty-eight. The fledgling actress was devastated; Aunt Ana had cared for her, believed in her, and encouraged her dreams. Now she was gone, and Maril was alone again...until a few days later when my father brought her home to meet his mother.

Nana helped fill the void created by Ana Lower's death. Maril could always turn to her for a sympathetic ear, a shoulder to cry on, and a heart full of wisdom and love. My grandmother became the orphan's mother for the rest of Maril's life.

* * *

Marilyn Monroe was driven to succeed, and I can reveal, from what I observed, absolutely nothing was going to stop her—not Harry Cohn, not anything. Yes, she cried after a setback and felt wounded for a short time, but she was a lovely, warm, indestructible hurricane of positive energy, and she was going to take everybody along for the ride, whether they liked it or not.

Daddy said she was one of the most intensely motivated voice students he ever worked with, and she made rapid progress under his instruction. She improved so quickly that, in August of '48, after just five months of voice lessons, Daddy urged her to try out for the Benny Goodman Orchestra. She did—and failed the audition. But my father's endorsement spoke volumes about her talent.

Daddy gave Marilyn Monroe the musical foundation to become an all-rounder on the big screen. Most actresses of her era—such as Deborah Kerr (*The King and I*), Natalie Wood (*West Side Story*), Audrey Hepburn (*My Fair Lady*), and Jeanne Crain (*Cheaper by the*

Dozen)—lip-synched their singing parts (most of which were voiced, without credit, by Marni Nixon). Maril, on the other hand, would handle her own parts—except for the falsetto "No, no, no, no, no, no, no… no!" in "Diamonds Are a Girl's Best Friend," dubbed by Gloria Wood.

While taking voice lessons with Daddy, Maril studied acting under Columbia's resident drama coach, Natasha Lytess. Maril would initially place certain friends, lovers, teachers, coaches, or doctors on a pedestal, seeing them as perfect individuals. When she discovered certain flaws she couldn't ignore, Maril's estimations of them unraveled.

On December 3, 1952, Natasha and Maril attended a Beverly Hills auction for Max Reinhardt's notebooks. Reinhardt's son Gottfried hoped to get them back. Consequently, Maril made one last offer as the hammer reached the table. Gottfried wrote to Maril to persuade her that he should have his father's notebooks. Although Maril considered donating them to a university, Natasha insisted she give the notebooks back to Gottfried. Maril agreed to give up the notebooks for the final price at auction. When Maril found out Gottfried and Natasha knew each other, Maril felt betrayed, realizing Natasha had placed Gottfried's interests over her own.

In 1956, Maril read an open page from her third husband Arthur Miller's journal during *The Prince and the Showgirl*, after which Arthur's fate had been sealed. According to Maril, Arthur wrote he had at first seen her as an angel and how his initial impression of her turned out to be wrong. Questioning Maril's monogamy, he concluded she was not as innocent as he thought she was, calling her a whore. Not unreasonably, she saw this as a massive betrayal of their marriage. Until the end of their marriage, Maril would act as if she was a wounded bird who never healed.

During the last two years of Maril's life, this unraveling would also happen to her last psychiatrist, Dr. Ralph Greenson, to the point where her trust in him withered. Once Maril understood that Greenson had hired housekeeper Eunice Murray as a spy to communicate her daily observations of Maril back to the psychiatrist, Maril felt double-crossed.

But with Freddie Karger, things were different. Maril always felt Daddy was brand new to her, as if she was reliving her first delightfully romantic encounter with him over and over again. The best way I can explain it is, in her mind, she viewed him like the coolest roller coaster in the theme park, never boring her.

As for the strange woman living with her across the street, Maril would quickly realize Natasha appeared as if she wanted to own every particle of her being under the guise of a teacher-pupil relationship. Time went on, and I could tell Daddy and Nana trusted Natasha less and less. Maril would get more irritable and sad after a long, harsh lesson from Natasha. In the end, this overbearing drama coach would ultimately have a huge impact on Maril's career—though not always for the best.

* * *

Ours was a show business family. My mother, father, and I lived in the heart of the Hollywood movie colony, close to Sunset Boulevard and Laurel Canyon. Hollywood was a beautiful place to live in those days, with clear skies and the fragrance of orange blossoms in the air. The Helms Bakery truck would rumble through our neighborhood, sounding its horn, calling people out of their homes to buy oven-warmed bread and pastries. Milk was delivered to our door, and our family physician, Dr. Jones, made house calls. It was a lovely way of life.

During the late 1940s and early '50s, our neighborhood was a who's who of Hollywood. Sydney Greenstreet lived on our block, his *Maltese Falcon* sidekick Peter Lorre was on the street behind us, and producer-director Stanley Kramer lived next door in a house that would later be occupied by Paul Douglas and his actress wife, Jan Sterling.

Meanwhile our next-door neighbor on the other side was actor-writer Morris Carnovsky, who, in 1951, courageously refused to testify before the House Un-American Activities Committee. The FBI once posted an agent in our home to spy on Mr. Carnovsky. As a fourth grader I thought this was very exciting. Unfortunately, he ended up being blacklisted and unable to work for a dozen years.

It's funny the things one remembers. I recall star Ricardo Montalbán sitting with us at Scandia's on the Sunset Strip talking about the high taxes. Thanks to our location, we hosted many celeb-filled parties—first at our house on Selma Avenue, just north of Sunset (where Mom, Daddy, and I lived before their separation) and later at Nana's house on North Harper Avenue. Some were black-tie events, and my parents always let me attend, wearing my best dress while watching the glitterati talk and laughing at grown-up jokes I didn't understand. Maril would often drop by at these parties. In 1950, she gave me an inscribed photograph of herself.

Marilyn Monroe by Frank Powolny in 1950, signed and inscribed by Marilyn Monroe: "To Terry, My little friend, Love Marilyn" (From the collection of Terry Karger)

One time, I was sitting next to Max Arnow, who was a talent scout for my favorite film, *Gone with the Wind* (1939). I was thrilled to hear his escapades during the time he was looking for the right actress to play Scarlett O'Hara.

One of our 1950s party guests was Daddy's best friend, Jack Lemmon. He was always very sweet to me, brushing my curls aside to kiss my forehead and call me "Fred's beautiful daughter." To me he was Uncle Jack, and I didn't know he was a famous actor until one day in 1955, when my family and I watched *Mister Roberts* in the theater. There, up on the screen, was the man with whom Daddy often smoked cigars and golfed at the Riviera Country Club—while joking that, being half Jewish like Mom, they actually belonged to "the Halfers' Club."

Freddie Karger with Jack Lemmon and Evelyn Keyes in 1954 (Columbia Pictures) (Photo by Lippman)

During this glamorous era, Daddy was always immaculately dressed in a lovely suit. He'd never step out of the house without his pocket handkerchief—even his undershorts were handmade! When I think of my father, I think kind, genteel, and refined. Many women adored him for his suave manner and his pearly white teeth. Yet, despite befriending many stars, he remained humble at heart.

* * *

Born in Boston, Massachusetts, Nana's real name was Anna (Ann) Florence Conley (June 13, 1886–November 13, 1975). Nana and her sister Effie (November 7, 1882–August 8, 1967) were the Conley Sisters of vaudeville, two beautiful Scotch-Irish girls with lovely singing voices.

They had a brother, John Conley, my great-uncle. Anna was the youngest of the three of them and Effie was the oldest. Uncle John and Joe Kennedy Sr. lived near each other, so he knew the Kennedys as kids growing up. They were friends when they were all just starting out, and later Joe and Uncle John went to Harvard together.

Effie was about thirteen when their mother died in Boston. Effie's mother used to sing for the opera and donate the money she made to charity.

Effie was a showgirl in vaudeville, a real character. She later married Fred Warren (September 16, 1880–December 5, 1940), who ran away from home in Illinois, and the two of them joined the vaudeville circuit. Their stage name became Warren & Conley. Fred and Effie Warren were trained musicians. He played piano, she did a song-and-dance routine, and they'd do one-liners. Next, the jugglers would come on with the dancing dog.

Nana retired from the vaudeville circuit when she married my grandfather Frederick Maxwell "Max" Karger Sr. An accomplished violinist with the Metropolitan Opera, Max cofounded Metro Pictures in 1915 to carve out a new career as a director and producer of silent films. Nana, meanwhile, became a grande dame of Hollywood society, attending Rudolph Valentino's weddings to Jean Acker in 1919 (held in Aunt Effie's backyard) and Natacha Rambova in 1923.

Her suite at the Hollywood Hotel welcomed all the great film personalities of that era, including Alla Nazimova, Mary Pickford, and her brother, Jack Pickford. So show business was very much part of the Karger family DNA.

(L): Photograph of Maxwell Karger, May 3, 1919,
issue of *The Moving Picture World*, p. 706
(R): Evans, photograph of Maxwell Karger, January
1920 issue of *Photoplay* magazine, p. 67

Max's buddies played a lot of poker at the Knickerbocker Hotel in Hollywood. If Max needed a stake for the poker games, he would borrow a piece of Nana's jewelry. If he lost, he would buy the jewelry back later and give it to her along with a new piece of jewelry. But Max was a pretty good player, so most times he easily won. Nana was a heck of a card player herself. She played four or five nights a week.

Once, Max was going on location in Arizona, and for a joke, the people at the film company made up a wanted poster saying, "Max Karger, Wanted." They all liked to play pranks on each other. A copy was sent to the sheriff of the town where they were going to shoot a film. The crew told the sheriff what train Max was arriving on, so when the train pulled into the station, they arrested Max as soon as he got off and took him to jail for the night. Of course, he was bailed out the next morning.

They were all friends and talk would eventually turn to poker. Nana had told us that she and Max and even the sheriff would join the games behind closed doors, although it was illegal to have money on the table.

Max's business slogan was "Do it now." He was known for his "Rooseveltian talk." Max's fascinated employees wrote down some of his epigrams:

- I don't want ideas; I want an audience.
- Do it the simplest way, the most natural way. We don't want nine reels of explanation; we want forty-five hundred feet of entertainment.
- Why lie when you can yell your way out?
- If you agree with me, I'll hate you; if you differ with me, I'll prove you're wrong.

In 1920, Charles Fox and Milton L. Silver of *Who's Who on the Screen* summarized Max's versatility throughout his life. They wrote:

> *Maxwell Karger, Metro's director general, was born in Ohio, reared a violinist and chose journalism for a career. However, he drifted from the newspaper field and became a dry goods clerk, advertising director for a big department store, floorwalker, leader of an orchestra, concert player, and finally a motion picture impresario. He played first violin with the Philharmonic and Metropolitan orchestras for seven years. After a romantic business and newspaper career, he came to New York and was one of the organizers of Metro. Mr. Karger believes in big things and does them. He is a creative executive with an imaginative turn-of-mind and seldom balks at an eighteen-hour day at the desk. He is an intensely enthusiastic film fan himself and sees a great future in the industry.*

Max had a beautiful home in Rye, New York, which was upper class. That's why Nana was able to live a nice life, because of what Max left her.

In those days, Metro Pictures had studios in New York and Los Angeles.

The Red Lantern (1919) as featured with the Nazimova Screen Production presented by Richard A. Rowland and Maxwell Karger with music by Fred Fisher (Metro Pictures Corporation) (From the collection of Terry Karger)

The Fatal Hour (1920) (From the collection of Terry Karger)

A Message from Mars (1921) (From the collection of Terry Karger)

In 1922, Max was on a train trip from the East Coast studio to the West Coast when he died of a massive heart attack. He was forty-six years old when he passed, making Nana, along with their daughter Mary and their son—my father, Fred, just five years old—the heirs to several million dollars.

A. J. Marik, January 16, 2001

Three years later, Metro was combined with Goldwyn Pictures and Louis B. Mayer Pictures to form MGM, the most powerful and respected motion picture studio of Hollywood's golden age.

Daddy inherited his musical talent from both Max and Nana, along with a love for entertaining people. He was amazingly gifted as pianist, songwriter, and vocal coach. Were it not for his help in improving her singing voice, the world might have never heard of Marilyn Monroe.

* * *

Before obtaining her law degree in January 1952, my mother, Patti Sacks Karger, was a showgirl and an actress. (You can see her in *Flying Down to Rio* with Fred Astaire and Ginger Rogers, as well as in *Man About Town* with Jack Benny.) She also performed at the Earl Carroll Theatre on Sunset Boulevard in the late 1930s. Carroll featured lavish Busby Berkeley–style productions on a revolving stage, with up to fifty showgirls backing the main performer. An illuminated sign at the entrance read, "Through these portals walk the most beautiful women in the world."

I have a photo of my mother in her showgirl costume with feathers and sequins. She hated it! She was somewhat embarrassed about her showgirl past, but I treasure that picture because she was so beautiful.

Patti Karger in her showgirl costume (From the collection of Terry Karger)

Mom didn't want to be known for her beauty but for her intellect and her legal skills. She had a photographic memory like President Kennedy and could flip through a book, then tell you all about it. A student of many religions, she had read the Bible from cover to cover, with many highlights and notes in the margins.

Studying law at the time of her separation and divorce from my father, Mom eventually became a prominent attorney, specializing in both entertainment law and celebrity divorces. My mother was one of the top two hundred female attorneys in the country. She was listed in *Who's Who* and did a lot of pro bono legal work. Mom and Debbie Reynolds helped start the Thalians charitable organization (the name comes from Thalia, the Greek muse of comedy and poetry), and my mom was actively involved. It was dedicated to improving mental health and is still operating today. Mom was glamorous and flamboyant, so it was only natural she and Maril would eventually become best friends (along with my Aunt Mary).

So, while Daddy wrote the music the stars sang and danced to, Mom fought many of their legal battles. Her law partner was Milton Cohen Jr. (whom she later married in Las Vegas) and, thanks to the firm of Cohen & Karger, some of the biggest Hollywood names visited our home and dropped into their law office: Cary Grant, Bing Crosby, FDR's son James Roosevelt, Clifford Heinz of the famous Heinz family, Claire Trevor, her husband Milton Bren (Claire's stepson is billionaire Donald Bren, president of the present-day Irvine Company of Orange County, California), even Leon Shamroy, the cinematographer who gave Maril her first screen test at Twentieth Century-Fox, and Duncan Renaldo, who became famous for playing the Cisco Kid on TV. Although I was very young, I remember what a true gentleman Mr. Renaldo was. I visited his ranch in the San Fernando Valley many times.

This was the world in which I was raised, so fame never impressed me. And it also didn't impress my family, which is why Maril felt so comfortable around us—not only when she first met us as an unknown contract player but also after she became one of the movie industry's brightest stars. To us, she was never a "screen goddess" or a "sex symbol." She was simply our Maril—sweet, soft, and a little shy.

During the first six months Daddy and Maril dated, we saw her all the time. When she wasn't working on her acting and singing, she'd often help Nana with chores and cooking or take her shopping. I loved having her around—and really liked how, instead of calling me Terry like everyone else, she'd address me by my initials, T.K.

Maril would take me to Wil Wright's ice cream parlor on Santa Monica Boulevard, not far from our house. It had red-and-white-striped awnings on the outside and red, white, and pink decor inside. Wil Wright's ice cream was richer, creamier, and sweeter than any other ice cream you could buy, and the selection was amazing, including chocolate mocha, peppermint stick, and pineapple pecan, served with little almond macaroons. Maril would order two hot fudge sundaes, then she and I would sit in wire-backed chairs at a marble-topped table, giggling as we ate and watched people outside passing by.

Without a doubt, Maril would have made a wonderful mother—and motherhood could have anchored her soul. Warm and affectionate toward me, always touching my hand or hugging me, she displayed love very differently than my mom, who just wasn't the soft, touchy-feely type. That's not a complaint about my mother, whose own love I never doubted; it's just an observation about how it compared to the aura of affection that radiated from Maril. The young actress was softer and, for me, easier to relate to, so I was really comfortable being around her. She demonstrated her affection via her words and her touch, and that's because Maril was a gentle spirit who spent her life searching for love after years of being abandoned and rejected. Then again, she was also a frightened lady who sometimes brooded about death. As she herself said:

> *Death figures in my dreams more than anything else. I often dream that I'm drowning, or being shot, or being hit by a car. As far back as I can remember, I've had an abnormal interest in death and the Hereafter. You've heard about me walking alone at night, but what I haven't told anyone before—you'll think I'm really crazy—is that walking in a graveyard after dark makes me recover from a fit of despondency or depression sooner than anything else… While I don't have any trouble sleeping once I drift off, I sometimes find it hard to get to sleep. Rattling doors and windows, crickets and things like that distract and disturb me, especially if I'm in one of my low blue moods.*[5]

Love could have saved Maril—the love of the right man or the mutual love of mother and child. She kept seeking love in the adoration of her fans as well as in the unblinking glass eye of the camera, but she confused it with success-based acclaim until she actually achieved the latter.

"Candle in the Wind," the song penned by Elton John and lyricist Bernie Taupin as a posthumous tribute to Marilyn Monroe, is beautiful, sad, and partly true. Not knowing who to turn to when life turns difficult is the untrue part. Maril knew where to go during the stormy times …

She held on to us as the first real family she ever knew, the family that loved her long before the world knew her name, the family who never would—and never did—abandon her.

2: SWEET AND GENEROUS

MARILYN MONROE'S AUTOBIOGRAPHY, *My Story*, devotes three entire chapters (15–17) to her romance with my father. In 1953, she began working on the book with Academy Award–winning screenwriter Ben Hecht. Maril met him on the set of Howard Hawks's 1952 comedy *Monkey Business*, in which she costarred with Cary Grant and Ginger Rogers (Hecht cowrote the screenplay). At that time, she was only twenty-eight years old.

Initially, Maril was excited about the book, and she and Hecht spent a lot of time on the project. However, she had less time and energy for it once her romance with baseball legend Joe DiMaggio took off in line with her career—which is why the book ended abruptly with their wedding and honeymoon.

My Story states up front that Maril wanted to protect the identity of my dad, whom she refers to only as "my lover"—though I have a hunch it was Hecht who changed the details to avoid a lawsuit. The chapter titled "My First Love" opens with this statement about my father: "He's married now to a movie star and it might embarrass him if I used his real name."

True enough—by that time Daddy was married to Academy Award–winning actress Jane Wyman. And Hecht altered many details to conceal Daddy's identity. The book stated that Maril and her lover met at MGM; no, they met at Columbia. It didn't mention that Maril's lover was a composer, bandleader, and her vocal coach at Columbia, only that he was a musician who "liked to play the piano."[6] And it also said Maril's lover had a six-year-old *son* at the time; no, he had a six-year-old *daughter*—me. I was an only child, and Daddy never had any other children. I understand why Hecht fudged the details, but I wish he hadn't changed my gender.

Though Ben Hecht did read an incomplete draft of *My Story* aloud to Maril, she never read or approved the final version eventually published a dozen years after her death.

* * *

Daddy taught Maril how to project her voice, breathe from the diaphragm, respond to the meaning of the lyrics, and move and gesture as a professional singer. During those private sessions, they fell in love. The feelings toward Daddy described in *My Story* were sweet, romantic, and intensely passionate.

Having entered Maril's life at a time when she felt like a failure following her dismissal from Twentieth Century-Fox, Daddy was her teacher, mentor, and in many ways the father figure she'd always longed for. Eleven years older, he represented strength and courage—qualities she felt she lacked.

"My lover was a strong individual," Maril wrote in *My Story*. "I don't mean he was dominant. A strong man doesn't have to be dominant toward a woman. He doesn't match his strength against a woman weak with love for him. He matches it against the world. When he came into my room and took me in his arms, all my troubles were forgotten. I even forgot Norma Jeane, and her eyes stopped looking out of mine. I even forgot about not being photogenic."[7]

Maril was describing the moment she and my father wordlessly acknowledged their mutual attraction—one evening at our house after Daddy had tucked me into bed. While she sat on the living room sofa, he seated himself at the grand piano and played her one song after another. She was enchanted, but what really impressed her was when he put on a pair of reading glasses. They made Fred look older, more fatherly. And they were Maril's undoing.

She hung on every note, every chord, every glance, every motion of his hands across the keys. Then, as the vibrations of the final chord hung in the air, he removed his glasses, rose from the piano, took Maril in his arms, and kissed her.

"My eyes closed," she'd recall, "and a new life began for me."[8]

Daddy made her feel *anything* was possible, and their love for one another changed everything.

* * *

When my mother and father were together, the three of us lived in a big, beautiful house at 8070 Selma Avenue in Laurel Canyon, just north of Sunset Boulevard, which is still there today. Then, after they separated, Daddy and I moved to Nana's house on North Harper while Mom rented out the Selma house and lived in a garage that she fixed up as a comfortable studio apartment—also on North Harper, less than a block away from Nana's. This was so, sharing joint custody, she could be close to me while studying at Southwestern Law School.

Soon after getting involved with Daddy, Maril began sharing a two-bedroom Romanesque villa apartment with Natasha Lytess and Natasha's infant daughter, Barbara, across the street from us. Referring to my father, Maril told reporter George Carpozi Jr. in 1955, "I'd been staying at the Studio Club, but I packed up and rented an apartment near his place and then every day he'd drop in on me. I could barely wait until he arrived. He'd come while he was on his way to work, or on the way home. I'd always be there for him."[9]

It may sound crazy that we all lived within a block of each other, but we really were one big happy family. Maril and Mom became best friends, as did Maril and Daddy's sister, Aunt Mary, who'd stay at our place with her children, Ben and Anne, for weeks at a time. Through my youthful eyes it seemed like a normal arrangement, but looking back now I'm amazed those relationships worked so well.

* * *

The Daddy-Maril romance lasted from the spring of 1948 to the spring of '49, but their friendship continued because she saw him as more than just her lover and vocal coach. He also taught her about life. In contrast to the roles Maril sometimes played, she was bright, thoughtful, and curious about the world, spending much of her spare time enjoying the classic books and classical music to which my father introduced her.

Despite dropping out of high school to marry her neighbor Jim at age sixteen, Maril was one of the smartest people I've ever known. Part of her insecurity was simply due to not finishing high school.

"Fear is stupid," she told journalist William J. Weatherby. "So are regrets. You know, for years I had this big regret that I hadn't gotten a high school diploma. What does it matter now?"[10]

Maril's lack of self-assurance made her appear shy and withdrawn at social gatherings—because she felt she had nothing to contribute to a conversation. But she was hungry to learn, and Daddy was a good teacher. Anything he was enthusiastic about, Maril was eager to explore.

Although my beautiful friend seemed to enjoy simple childhood games as much as I did, Maril had an inquisitive and thoughtful mind. She thought deeply about God, the soul, and human existence. Maril said years later, "I know that I could prevent myself from becoming ill and from going into emotional tailspins if I had the time to sit quietly and meditate, and by prayer achieve peace of mind."[11]

And she became an avid reader of Sigmund Freud, hoping to understand some of her own emotional wounds while discussing the writers and artists she admired.

One of Maril's favorite pastimes was to rummage around the Pickwick bookstore, opening books at random pages to read a few paragraphs. She'd buy the books she liked; fiction, nonfiction, poetry—categories didn't matter to her. It was all about what appealed to her at the moment. Inquisitive, grasping ideas very quickly, Maril picked up books as if they were intellectual prizes to be devoured and explored. Always on the lookout, she'd often ask me what I was reading.

Daddy helped fuel the obsession with improving her mind. And others—including Natasha Lytess and, later, third husband Arthur Miller—would also influence her reading choices as well as her thinking. But Maril's own inner drive was, ultimately, the most important factor.

* * *

In *My Story*, Maril talked about how forthright and demanding my father could be. However, when he criticized her, it was only to help her learn and grow—a teacher challenging his student...or a parent admonishing a child. The fact is, for all her sexuality, there were child-like gaps in Maril's understanding of the world.

Some things Daddy said must have seemed harsh to her—especially given how the line between teacher and lover probably became blurred in her mind. Yet, well aware how determined she was to succeed in Hollywood, he wanted to prepare her for the harsh realities of the life she'd chosen.

"I never complained about his criticism," Maril later recalled, "but it hurt me." With the benefit of hindsight, she knew what my father had to say "was sort of true."[12]

The biggest hurdle Maril faced in becoming a singer and actress was stage fright. After witnessing the terrible insecurity that threatened her stardom-based ambitions, Daddy took Maril to some Hollywood friends' dinner parties where, sitting at the piano, he'd accompany her singing of the numbers they'd rehearsed at the studio.

Bob Hope's personal photographer Murray Garrett took countless shots of Maril and considered her incredibly photogenic—as well as intensely afraid.

"I started taking pictures of Marilyn before she was famous," Mr. Garrett recalled. "Nobody really knew who she was at that point. She was staying at a house called the Studio Club in Hollywood that had a bunch of models living there. She was one of them. I took her to the beach one day and photographed her and paid her twenty-five bucks to pose for what was then called cheesecake. She was wearing a two-piece bathing suit. That was the first experience I had with Marilyn. And that was at the beginning, when I first met her. Then I followed up after she began her movie career.

"Because I was covering Hollywood, I had great exposure to Marilyn at premieres. In your lifetime as a photojournalist, you run across certain people and you realize you almost have to *try* to take a bad picture of them. Marilyn was like the Cary Grant of women; you just couldn't get a bad picture of her. There are certain people with that gift. Certainly, George Clooney is one of them now. When you look at the history of motion pictures, there are very few people who fall into that category. I always described her as a deer in the headlights. Here was this woman who wanted more than anything in the world to have this kind of career. And when she got it, she was scared to death. You could smell the fear. She loved it yet she was scared of it."

Over time, Maril gained the confidence to better manage her fears. The terror was always there, hidden behind her wide eyes and dazzling smile, but she learned to channel it to energize her performance. What an awful existence; desperate for success, she felt she'd die without it—and knew she'd have to endure overwhelming fear to achieve it.

With Daddy's coaching and encouragement, Maril made progress controlling her fears, but she never conquered them. Instead, her performance anxiety increased over time, and I recall her telling me her lateness arriving on film sets was due to her fear of going in front of the cameras.

Daddy saw the fierce ambition and abject terror in Maril, each battling for control. Cognizant of her talent as well as her beauty, he wanted her ambition to win out over the fear—and hoped his critiques would toughen her for the challenges ahead. He didn't want her to be yet another Hollywood casualty.

* * *

I've read how our family, including Nana, wanted Daddy to marry Maril—and how he, in a jealous rage, purportedly begged her to do so after she started dating her agent, Johnny Hyde. When she declined, he then enlisted Nana to change her mind—but these stories were patently untrue. Daddy never begged Maril to marry him. And, according to my cousin Johnny, "Auntie Ann would never have begged Marilyn to marry Fred. That's not the way she was."

"Based upon the evidence and conversations with both Freddie and his mother, he had no intention of ever marrying her," agreed biographer Fred Lawrence Guiles. "He put up resistance to the idea all along the line, and nothing Marilyn could do or say would change his mind... The immediate result of Freddie's wall of reserve with Marilyn was to make Marilyn more determined than ever to win his love and affection."[13]

The bottom line: Maril just wasn't Daddy's type. He, I'd later understand, was attracted to strong, independent women; whereas my mother Patti Sacks and stepmother Jane Wyman were very confident and strong-willed, Maril was too needy and too sexy. As a kid, I myself noticed her wearing tight clothing without underwear, but at that age I didn't really think about it.

Daddy also noticed, and he didn't approve. Maril's lack of inhibition was another problem for my father. He wasn't a prude, but he did have a strong sense of propriety and moral boundaries. I got the impression Maril intimidated Daddy with how she dressed. It bothered him tremendously. She liked the attention in an innocent sort of way, men inevitably stared, and he really didn't appreciate it.

Concealed in her headscarf disguise, she could go almost anywhere without being recognized. Yet she didn't hide the figure, face, or magnetic effect she had on the opposite sex. Even if they didn't know who she was, men would invent excuses to introduce themselves. She'd call them wolves—prompting me to imagine them salivating, with tongues wagging like in the cartoons.

I did see some wolf approaches when Maril and I were out together. She had a polite but firm technique for turning them away.

"Here, take my business card."

"No, thanks. I have enough."

"Call me."

"Sorry, I don't have a phone."

"Then call me when you get one."

"I can't."

"Why?"

"I don't want to."

Continuing on her way, she'd remain unscathed and unrecognized.

Those days when Maril picked me up from school, took me out for ice cream, hugged me, and told me she loved me are indelibly imprinted in my memory. Also relating to my cousins by getting down on their level, she would have made a wonderful stepmother. And had she experienced the motherhood she'd always longed for, she might have never needed pills and alcohol to numb her pain.

Once, shortly before my seventh birthday, I went window-shopping with Daddy and Maril—and saw the most beautiful blue dress with a white bow in a store window.

"Daddy, look at that dress! Isn't it pretty?"

"Yes, honey. Very pretty."

"Would you buy it for my birthday? *Please?*"

"It's kind of expensive. Maybe next year."

A few days later, at my birthday party, Maril and our family gathered around me as I opened presents—including one box that made me gasp. Inside it was the blue dress with the big white bow. Surprised and thrilled, I was about to thank Daddy when I read the card:

> *Happy Birthday, T.K.!*
> *I can't wait to see you in this.*
> *Love,*
> *Maril*

Her generosity means more to me today than it did back then because I'm now aware of how little money she had—and how much she must have loved me to make such a sacrifice.

Then again, early in his relationship with Maril, Daddy arranged for her to visit Dr. Walter Taylor, the cosmetic orthodontist to the stars who was responsible for many movie-screen smiles during the '30s and '40s. The only imperfection in her gorgeous features was a slight protrusion of her front teeth. This was a simple matter to fix with a retainer, and Dr. Taylor took care of it for free as a favor to my father.

Yes, Daddy could be critical of Maril, and his words sometimes hurt her feelings, but she knew that he cared for her.

* * *

Nana always had friends (including Maril) over for dinner parties. After dinner one time, we were in the living room. The grown-ups swapped stories, and my cousins and I sat on the floor and listened.

At one point, Maril asked Nana's guests, "Have you met my dog, Fang?"

"You have a dog…named Fang?"

Maril smiled. "My guard dog. I take her everywhere—for protection, you know. Here, Fang!"

"But—"

"Come on, girl! Here, Fang!"

"Fang" sped out of the hallway and into the living room. With that name, we were all expecting a much bigger dog. Maril loved to prank people. "Fang," of course, was Josefa, Maril's short-haired Chihuahua.

Marilyn Monroe with her dog Josefa by Earl Leaf in 1950

The dog had been a gift from Joseph Schenck (who cofounded Twentieth Century-Fox with Darryl Zanuck), and Maril named her after Mr. Schenck. Josefa scampered around the room, yip-yip-yipping and sniffing at everyone—then she leaped into Maril's lap, trembling and looking around the room with dark, anxious eyes.

Josefa may not have been much of a guard dog, but she was adorable. We all loved playing with her, and Maril doted on her. She was fond of nicknaming people and pets. She would call her little dog Joseffer around my cousins and me.

* * *

Maril celebrated Christmas 1948 with our family because, following the death of Ana Lower—and the confinement of her mother to a mental health facility—she had no other relatives with whom to spend the holidays. Seeing her with Daddy, his ex-wife, and the rest of the

family nevertheless didn't seem strange; my parents had divorced ami-
cably, Maril hadn't been a factor, and so jealousy was never an issue.

Many of the presents under Nana's Christmas tree were for me.
When Maril noticed that my cousins Ben and Anne didn't have as
many, she bought some additional gifts so they wouldn't feel left out.
I'm sure her orphanage years made her especially sensitive to their feelings. And, judging by how she sang Christmas carols with us around
Nana's grand piano, without the breathy bedroom voice, I knew there
was a lot of Norma Jeane in our Maril but very little Marilyn Monroe.

That Christmas, one gift from her didn't end up under Nana's tree.
Bought for Daddy—and accorded a full chapter in Maril's autobiography—its story began, oddly enough, with her brief but memorable
appearance in the Marx Brothers movie *Love Happy*. She'd auditioned
for it a few weeks after parting ways with Columbia and had been
approved by Groucho, Harpo, and independent film producer Lester
Cowan when, watching her overtly sexy walk, Groucho asserted she
was "Mae West, Theda Bara, and Bo Peep all rolled into one."[14]

By December, Maril wanted to get something special for my
father—something expensive—but she was broke. Then, one morning, Louella Parsons's column in the *Los Angeles Examiner* reported
that Lester Cowan was placing her under contract. As this was the
first she'd heard about it, Maril hurried to Cowan's office, asked him if
it was true, and learned he would indeed be signing her…after decid-
ing how much to pay.

Walking on air as she left Cowan's office, Maril dropped into a
jewelry store, showed the proprietor the Louella Parsons clipping, and
assured him that, although she didn't have two dimes to rub together,
she'd soon be making good money as an actress. If the jeweler would
trust her, she'd like to buy an expensive gift for someone dear. When
the jeweler agreed, Maril selected a $500 gold watch.

That was a *lot* of money in those days, but she wasn't trying to
buy Daddy's affection; she just had a big heart. And she also gave him
a telling answer when, handed the gift after she ran straight to our

house, he turned the watch over and asked why her name hadn't been engraved on it.

"Because you'll leave me someday and you'll have some other girl to love," she replied. "You wouldn't be able to use my present if my name was on it."[15]

Maril continued to make payments on that watch long after her romance with my father had ended. And she spoke candidly in her autobiography about her love for him—and her heartbreak. She knew Daddy cared for her, but what did he really mean when he'd said he loved her?

My Story described how that love had pulled her up from the "bottom of the ocean," how she'd absorbed strength from him, how her heart ached for him, and how her knees went weak at his touch. Yet my father didn't seem to love her the way she loved him—waiting for hours at her apartment, hoping he'd call, eager to meet him anytime, anyplace. Unavailable for days, he never seemed to mind their time apart. And whereas she would have readily married him, he was reticent.

"I was torn myself and wondered, 'Could it work?'" Daddy once pondered. "Her ambition bothered me to a great extent. I wanted a woman who was a homebody. She might have thrown it all over for the right man."[16]

Talking with journalist Jane Wilkie, drama coach Natasha Lytess recalled a conversation she'd had with Maril concerning my father:

"One day she told me she was in love and miserable because the man would not marry her. His name was not mentioned. I learned later the man was Freddie Karger at Columbia. I tried to help. I told her if he treated her this way he was not worth her tears."[17]

The last person to interview Maril before her death was writer-photographer George Barris. "I don't think very much of Fred," Mr. Barris remarked. "The mere fact that he refused to marry her I think is very discouraging because she was very much in love with him. Of course, I know Fred's mother and the family were very close to her. She was heartbroken. He broke her heart, period. Fred was quoted as saying he didn't think she would make a good mother, and I think that's very disheartening. He didn't think she was a nice person for a child. How can he have that feeling towards a young woman who was in love with him?"

If George Barris had known my father beyond what he read in *My Story*, he would have realized Fred Karger was trying to make the best decision for me—as well as for Maril. Daddy genuinely cared for her. And even after concluding they weren't right for each other, he continued to encourage her, build her confidence, and help advance her career.

For her part, in love with my father on so many levels—romantically, artistically, intellectually—Maril was heartbroken when informed he wouldn't marry her. She loved him the way a protégé loves a demanding mentor, because he cared enough to teach her, coach her, and challenge her. Daddy devoted a lot of his own time to rehearsals with Maril, building her confidence as a performer—and she loved him for believing in her. So she cried when he broke the news to her.

Here was a woman who was really in love with my dad. She would have jumped off the tallest bridge if she thought they had a chance of being together. That's how much she loved him. And I really loved *her*, which is why, to this day, I still miss her deeply. I would have been thrilled to have Maril as my stepmother, but Daddy knew his own heart, his own mind, and had his own reasons. He had to do what he thought was right. And I respect his decision.

"If one person truly loved me and I was sure of it, all my troubles would be over," Maril once said.[18]

I wish she had found the love she searched for all her life, the love that eluded her. And I wish she had found that love with Daddy.

Even after he made it clear to Maril that marriage wasn't in his plans, they continued to enjoy each other's company. Daddy often took her out to clubs on the Sunset Strip or for dinner and dancing in Malibu. One time they drove to Virginia City, east of Lake

Tahoe, to explore the Old West town and go dancing at the Bucket of Blood Saloon.

Meanwhile, they also took me along on some of their trips: to the beaches at Santa Monica and Malibu, where we rode on big, inflated, pillow-shaped floats in the ocean; to Santa Barbara to explore the botanical garden and visit the mission; and to Anza-Borrego to see the California desert wildflowers. The hills were ablaze with desert dandelions, poppies, and lupines, and Maril was delighted by the passing scenery. She looked at the world with childlike wonder.

When she and my father clicked, it was beautiful. When they fought, I learned relationships weren't always magical. How was I supposed to know? I was just a kid learning about life while it unfolded in front of me—and this undoubtedly helped when, later on, I began dating.

Besides taking her out on the town after they broke up, Daddy lent Maril his car and coached her performances. She, meanwhile, still came to our home, shared meals with us, played with my cousins and me, and helped Nana in the kitchen or around the house. Nana sometimes mended Maril's clothes, and they often had heart-to-heart talks.

Maril put her arms around the Kargers, and we put ours around her. For the rest of her life, she sent Nana gifts and a card on her birthday, as well as a dozen red roses every Mother's Day. That in itself spoke to who she was and how she felt about our family.

3: BIG SCREEN INGÉNUE

FEBRUARY 10, 1949: MARIL and our family went to see *Ladies of the Chorus* at the Carmel Theater on Santa Monica Boulevard.

Wearing dark glasses, no makeup, and a scarf on her head, she watched the entire film slumped in her seat, fearing—somewhat hopefully—she might be recognized. It was a convincing disguise. This movie was a thinly disguised retelling of the Cinderella fairy tale, with Maril in that role while her burlesque-queen mom, Adele Jergens, was basically her fairy godmother.

Although Jergens was the star, Maril was thrilled to see her name on the theater marquee—unaware that, once she'd become a star, Columbia would rerelease the picture with Marilyn Monroe top-billed in the opening credits.

It was the first time I saw Maril up on the big screen—which is probably why I remember my ticket cost sixteen cents. Watching her sing, dance, and get into a hair-pulling catfight with another dancer, I said a bit too loudly, "You should get an Oscar," prompting her to giggle, put a finger to her lips, and lean close to whisper, "I wouldn't be on that screen if it wasn't for your daddy. He's a wonderful teacher."

When we exited through the lobby, nobody who'd just watched Marilyn Monroe in the musical romance recognized her in real life. "Isn't it amazing?" Aunt Mary exclaimed outside the theater. "No one knows who you are."

"In the movie, I'm Marilyn Monroe," came the knowing reply. "Out here, I'm still Norma Jeane."

Terry Karger

As my cousin Ben D'Aubery observed, Maril could adopt and remove her Marilyn Monroe persona at will:

"She was drop-dead gorgeous, even when walking down the street unrecognized as Norma Jeane, but everybody noticed her the moment she became 'Marilyn.' That was strictly a character she invented; it wasn't *her*, which proves how good of an actress she was."

During those early years, I always felt Maril knew who she was—and who she wasn't. She clearly knew where Norma Jeane left off and Marilyn Monroe began. Later on, when stardom took hold, I sometimes wondered if Norma Jeane hadn't got lost somewhere inside the image.

* * *

"What would you like to be when you grow up?" Maril often asked me when I was seven. My answer changed every time: if she bought me a Popsicle, I'd want to drive an ice cream truck; if we'd just seen a movie, I might want to be a spy or a doctor.

One time, however, I pleased her by saying, "I want to be an actress like you."

"If that's what you choose to do, I'm sure you'll be a fine actress."

"When did *you* decide to be an actress?"

"When I was a little older than you are now. I thought it would be wonderful to pretend to be anyone, to live at any time or any place in history."

One time I said, "I want to be a teacher."

"I think you'd make a great teacher, T.K.," was Maril's characteristic response. And those words must have resonated within me, because I'd eventually acquire an education degree and teach for twenty-eight years.

Maril loved being around children because their love was unconditional. A child didn't care if she was famous; a child wouldn't want to exploit or take advantage of her. The children would invariably reciprocate the attention and affection she'd given to them.

- 42 -

I remember Maril playing hide-and-seek in our big backyard with my cousins and me. Spotting wisps of blonde hair floating in the breeze from behind a tree when I was "it," I called her out. Only years later did I realize she was always the last to be found when any of the big kids were "it" and—by hiding in obvious places—the first to be found when little kids like me were "it."

Age-wise, Maril was like an aunt to me. Yet, being uninhibited and childlike (in the best sense of that word), she often seemed more like a big sister than a grown-up—as well as a confidante in ways my parents could never be. Sure, they'd always tell me I could talk to them about anything, anytime, but some things I'd keep to myself rather than risk upsetting them or getting lectured.

I didn't know how to talk to my parents about their divorce without making them feel bad, but I could talk to Maril about it. She didn't pretend to listen to me; she actually listened—and I did the same when this young woman who'd felt so alone in foster homes and an orphanage needed someone to talk to.

"Terry, I know it hurts to have your mother and father living apart," she once said, "but at least your mother is close by and your father loves you. I barely know my mother and I never knew my father at all. I would never want a child of mine to go through what I went through. You have a big, wonderful family; be grateful for such a blessing."

Whenever Maril and my dad were together, I could see the love in her eyes and in the way she'd gently touch his shoulder. It was as if she had to keep that love close to her to prevent it from slipping away. Even when she was having a really bad week, his smile would bring her back to life. Maril loved Daddy so much, she tried her best to avoid offending him and, when their relationship was at its height, she'd do anything to make him happy.

"What do you like most about my dad?" I recall asking her.

"Your father's got a very attractive smile and beautiful eyes. I love looking into them."

Still, I knew Maril wasn't just in love with Daddy's eyes and smile. She admired him for his class and for the confidence she gained by being around him.

"It's a man's inner strength, his spirit, which appeals to me," Maril would publicly explain years later. "Women, very much like men, tend to be attracted to the obvious—muscles or good looks. You can include me in, up to a point, on that. But it's that something which doesn't show on the surface, which appeals to me. Call it character, or what you will."[19]

After they'd been together for a while, I really thought Daddy and Maril would get married. I certainly wanted them to; when it didn't happen, I couldn't understand why. If ever there was a woman on the planet who was irresistible to men, it was Marilyn Monroe. And of all the men in Maril's life, Fred Karger was the first one she truly, passionately loved—yet he was the only one who ultimately resisted her charm.

* * *

There were five children in our extended family: Aunt Mary's children, Anne and Ben; my cousins Johnny and Jacqui Warren, who often came to visit; and me, the youngest of the bunch. Maril loved spending time with all of us.

"I met Marilyn in 1948, when I was seven," Johnny recalls. "She came with Freddie to our house on Valley Vista in Sherman Oaks. They were romantically involved, and she glowed around him. Marilyn passionately loved Fred. It wasn't my own gut feeling…everybody felt it. And I knew she loved kids by the way she hugged me. I remember Marilyn bending down to kiss me and I was so shy, I kind of pulled back. 'Nice meeting you, Johnny,' she said. It was sweet. I'll never forget that particular moment. Here was this lady holding me, wanting to be very warm and friendly."

Johnny also remembers how everything changed after her breakthrough role as the sultry Rose Loomis in *Niagara* made her a star:

"All of a sudden, the whole world was excited and clamoring for her. How strange to be held sweetly one day by this lovely lady friend of Uncle Fred's; then, suddenly, the whole universe is shouting her name, wanting to take hold of her. Still, even with her newfound fame, Marilyn never changed around us. A dear, beautiful, sweet gal, so different than what the world saw or what she was portrayed as on the screen. Very sharp, very intelligent.

"I remember Maril getting up in her nightgown and having coffee and breakfast with us. She was just one of the family. She needed a family and we filled that gap for her life. She was so loving to us, and when I was a little guy, she'd hold me. I felt I was sort of like her child.

"We got to know her very well. In fact, all the way through her career she would hang out at our house to get away from publicity. It was a special kind of relationship we had. The kids in our family were told to never tell anyone that she came to our house. We honored that so she could come by and stay a few days and enjoy her privacy. Nobody said anything and we were always sorry to see her go.

"One day, newspaper people showed up at our door, asking, 'Was Marilyn Monroe here?' I don't know how they found out, but we protected Marilyn. We played dumb. 'Marilyn who?'"

* * *

Maril took me to Christian Science Sunday school. Nana and Daddy had ensured I was baptized in the Catholic Church, but Mom was a Christian Scientist like Maril, who, when we first got to know her, was very serious about it. No stimulants, including coffee or tea; no depressants. Only when the pressures of stardom increased would she quit adhering to the Christian Science teachings of Aunt Ana and rely increasingly on alcohol and pills.

Maril often stayed at our home even when Daddy was at the studio. Ben and Anne lived with us during that summer of 1948; one day, nine-and-a-half-year-old Ben was about to grab his baseball bat and glove from the closet in Daddy's room when, opening the door, he stopped in his tracks. There, seated in front of the dresser mirror, was Maril, putting on her makeup—in the nude.

"Sorry, I was looking for my baseball bat."

Staring directly into the mirror, Maril said, "Come on in and get it, Ben."

Decades later, Ben recalled, "I came in and got my baseball bat and glove, and left, not knowing what I was looking at because I was too young."

Maril had an unconventional attitude toward nudity, going back to childhood. In her autobiography, she recalled sitting in church while everyone sang, fighting the impulse to throw off her clothes and stand up naked—while asking God to stop her. As she herself explained, this was prompted by loneliness and a related need for attention.

Maril's nude fantasies came without any sense of guilt or shame. Instead, they countered the shame of being a poor orphan, forced to wear hand-me-down clothes.[20]

"I dress from the feet up," she told a reporter. "I start out nude and then put on my shoes and stockings. I love nude-colored shoes because they make me feel like I'm walking on my toes. I never wear nail polish because there's more of a nude feeling without it. Maybe I shouldn't say nude. Maybe I should say I just don't like being fenced in. I sleep in the nude, between very thin sheets and under a down-filled, satin comforter—nude colored."[21]

Nudity, of course, had a significant impact on Maril's career. Following the termination of her Columbia contract and appearance in *Love Happy*, she was out of work and out of prospects. By the spring of 1949, Maril was behind in her rent and needed fifty dollars.

A year earlier, under contract at Fox, Maril had been asked to pose nude by photographer Tom Kelley. At first, she'd refused, fearing it might hurt her career...until impending poverty persuaded her she had little to lose. In May of '49 she called Kelley, was offered fifty bucks for just three hours' work, and subsequently posed naked against a red satin backdrop—while his wife was there as an assistant.

Just seven years old, I knew nothing about that photo shoot—and I doubt Maril mentioned it to Daddy around the time they were ending their affair. Nevertheless, when her nude image appeared on a calendar, she was terrified the scandal would sink her career.

"Her religious upbringing with Aunt Ana, a churchgoing Christian Scientist, had taught her that truth would overcome anything," said photographer and friend George Barris. "That is why Marilyn Monroe eventually told all. The truth saved her pride and her career. Her fans loved her more than ever for her honesty."[22]

Another of Maril's friends, Hollywood gossip columnist Sidney Skolsky, helped obtain her an interview with Aline Mosby, the film industry reporter for *United Press International*. When Mosby broke the backstory behind the nude calendar, it appeared in newspapers across the country:

> *A photograph of a beautiful nude blond on a 1952 calendar is hanging in garages and barbershops all over the nation. Marilyn Monroe admitted today that the beauty is she... In 1949 she was just another scared young blonde, struggling to find fame in the magic city, and all alone. As a child she lived in a Hollywood orphanage. She was pushed around among 12 sets of foster parents before she turned an insecure 16. After an unsuccessful marriage, she moved into Hollywood's famed Studio Club, home of hopeful actresses. "I was a week behind on my rent," she explained. "I had to have the money."*[23]

Mosby gave the story a sympathetic slant, portraying Maril as a young woman in a tough spot who disrobed for the camera just to survive. This helped shape public reaction; instead of condemning her as a threat to public morals, people cheered her pluck and determination—and she became more popular than ever thanks to the invaluable publicity selling even more movie tickets and exposing her talent as an actress.

While Maril thanked Mosby for saving her career, all she ever earned from those calendars was the original fifty-dollar modeling fee—but at least it enabled her to pay her rent.

* * *

Just as Maril wasn't self-conscious about her own nudity, she took male exhibitionists in stride. On the street next to ours was an apartment building where an odd character named Arthur Markman lived. Arthur had made himself quite popular with the ladies of the neighborhood during World War II. In those days, silk and nylon were in short supply, so ladies' stockings were strictly rationed and very hard to get. Arthur would steal stockings and make them available to women in the neighborhood. Lacking any sense of boundaries—property or social—he'd often take a shortcut through our backyard when walking to and from his home. It was annoying but harmless…until the occasion when, noticing Maril there, Arthur walked over to her, put out his hand to introduce himself—and sucked in his gut to ensure his pants fell to his ankles.

"Um, you dropped something," she said, nonplussed, before walking into the house, leaving Arthur with his pants—and his jaw—on the ground. Maril was totally unfazed.

Yet she did have major misgivings about Natasha Lytess, complaining to Daddy and Nana about how her roommate and drama coach had attached herself in a Svengali-like way that went beyond a normal teacher-student relationship. It was as if she wanted the young actress to be completely dependent on her.

Natasha had helped Maril develop her talents early on, but while my father tried to build Maril's confidence so she'd become more self-assured, Natasha seemed determined to tear that confidence down. Maril felt she could scarcely make a move or speak a line without her coach on the set—and the result was an acting style that adhered to Natasha's insistence on unnaturally precise diction.

In some of her early films, not including *Ladies of the Chorus*, Maril enunciated her words with self-conscious precision. Several directors suggested she speak more naturally, but Natasha wouldn't have it; those diction habits were here to stay, and while they'd be part of Marilyn Monroe's unique charm in lighthearted films like *Gentlemen Prefer Blondes* and *How to Marry a Millionaire*, they'd also prove to be a hindrance in more dramatic pictures such as *River of No Return*.

Nana's brother, my Uncle John, liked to kid Maril whenever she practiced her diction around the Karger family. "My name is Marilyn," she'd announce with much affectation. "It is *very* nice to meet you."

"Shouldn't you say, 'My name's Marilyn, it's great to meet ya!'" he'd respond.

We all knew she wasn't trying to be pretentious—and in time she'd come to realize Natasha's ideas about acting were holding her back and hurting her self-confidence. Unfortunately, the acting coaches who'd replace her would probably do even more damage.

* * *

In 1950, having caught an eyeful of Marilyn's steaming-hot appearance opposite Groucho Marx in *Love Happy*, the Marine Corps asked her to perform at Air Station El Toro, near Irvine, California. Naturally, she accepted—although, nervous about singing live in front of a raucous all-male audience, she asked Daddy to accompany her for moral support.

As things turned out, Maril overcame her initial stage fright to give a brilliant performance. A thousand Marines fell in love with her—and Daddy was impressed by how she'd grown in terms of her confidence and onstage presence. What's more, he felt vindicated: the tough things he'd said to her since she'd started taking lessons with him in early 1948—things she felt were hurtful—had apparently paid off. And the same could soon be said for Natasha Lytess introducing her to Russian literature.

After reading works by Leo Tolstoy, Anton Chekhov, and Fyodor Dostoevsky, Maril was especially drawn to the character of Grushenka in Dostoevsky's *The Brothers Karamazov*. A beautiful twenty-two-year-old temptress with the power to stir lust in every man she meets,

Grushenka eventually undergoes a profound spiritual transforma-tion. This role could have been written for Marilyn—which is why, when MGM subsequently started planning a screen adaptation of *The Brothers Karamazov*, she asked agent Johnny Hyde to secure it for her.

As Maril would tell future *Village Voice* cofounder John Wilcock in 1953:

> *People made fun of me when I said I wanted to play* The Brothers Karamazov. *People did funny imitations of me—and incidentally, I'm flattered that anybody would imitate me—but it's still my dream role to play the part of Grushenka... I feel more serious about this than anything else in the world. I want to be a good actress. If I ever know I'm good, I shan't care what people say about me. Some people say I'm a dumb blonde. I suppose they're entitled to their opinion... It doesn't really matter what people say about you. If it's wrong, it's bound to hurt a bit, but it won't alter things. You know, yourself, how things really are.*[24]

Much to Maril's sadness, *The Brothers Karamazov* would finally reach the screen in February 1958—with Austrian-Swiss actress Maria Schell in the role Maril had coveted.

4: THE TWO JANES

ONE EVENING IN MID-1952, I watched Marilyn Monroe stand in front of a mirror at our home and remove her makeup to revert back to Maril. Tousling her blonde hair, she covered it with a headscarf and put on a pair of large sunglasses to ensure no one would recognize her out on the street.

"Where are you going?"

"Grauman's Chinese Theatre to see *Son of Paleface*."

"All by yourself? Why?"

"There's an actress I want to check out: Jane Russell. We've met before, but she and I are gonna be in a picture called *Gentlemen Prefer Blondes*."

At this point, Maril had already achieved her breakthrough in the noir thriller *Niagara*, filmed in 1952, released in January 1953. Giving her top billing for the first time, it was a huge box office hit, yet *Variety* reported that several women's groups were condemning Marilyn's "frank characterization" in the film.

"I played a tramp in that picture," she conceded, "but I was only acting. It would be awfully silly if people thought you were whatever you played in movies. I don't want to be a millionaire, and yet I played in that movie about how to marry one."[25]

On the *Niagara* set during a break in filming, a young fan named Mike Petix took two candid never-before-published snapshots of Maril and his friends.

Marilyn Monroe by Mike Petix in June 1952
(From the collection of Jay Margolis)

"He lived in Buffalo, just over ten miles from Niagara Falls," Joe Petix recalls about his late Uncle Mike. "When he heard Marilyn was coming to town to shoot a movie, he and a few friends went there and got to be extras. He told me she was more beautiful in person than on screen and she was very, very nice."

The next two Marilyn films released in 1953—*Gentlemen Prefer Blondes* and *How to Marry a Millionaire*—were even bigger hits than *Niagara*, cementing her status as box office gold. Yet, even though it was Maril the public clamored to see, her costars made the big money.

Marilyn Monroe by Frank Powolny in 1953, signed and inscribed by Marilyn Monroe: "To Terry, My love, Marilyn" (From the collection of Terry Karger)

Maril's contracted $1,250 weekly salary meant she earned between $15,000 and $18,000 per picture, while Jane Russell received $200,000 for *Gentlemen Prefer Blondes* and Betty Grable was paid $150,000 for *How to Marry a Millionaire*. Sure, Maril was no longer poor, but she also wasn't rich by Hollywood standards—and she never would be, requiring a mortgage to purchase her first home, a Spanish-style bungalow, during the last year of her life.

In *Gentlemen Prefer Blondes*, wearing a shocking-pink dress against a lush red backdrop, Marilyn wowed audiences with her iconic performance of "Diamonds Are a Girl's Best Friend." It quickly became her signature song, but the attendant fame never went to her head.

Instead, Tinseltown's biggest, most bankable star continued to seek Nana's advice, help her around the house, and act like a playful big sister toward me and my cousins.

Jane Russell first met Maril when Maril was only sixteen. Jane recalled, "I knew her first husband Jim Dougherty because we went to high school together. Marilyn was with him one time, and he said, 'I want you to meet my new wife.' She had been with a foster family. Because the family was moving out of the state, Jim married her."

Years later, Jane had fond memories of Maril while making *Gentlemen Prefer Blondes*: "I was still in the makeup chair when Marilyn's makeup man told mine that Marilyn was all ready. She had come in at least an hour before I did. Marilyn just felt nervous about going out alone. I'd go by her dressing room and say, 'Come on, Baby, we've got about ten minutes to go.' She'd look up at me and say, 'Oh, all right,' and we'd trot on out together."

Was Maril's chronic lateness to the set due to her being temperamental and uncooperative? Not at all. She was paralyzed by stage fright—and nobody in the cast and crew understood her terror or tried to help her.

"Those other idiots would just sit there and sulk because she was late," Ms. Russell explained, "but nobody went by to get her."

What about press reports that Jane Russell and Marilyn Monroe hated each other?

"It wasn't that way at all. She was like a little sister to me. She was very sweet and got very upset about a lot of things that I wouldn't have gotten upset about at all. But this was Marilyn."

Sympathizing with Maril because of her childhood hurts, Jane recalled Tommy Noonan—who played Lorelei Lee's wealthy fiancé—talking to a friend on the set of *Gentlemen Prefer Blondes*. "Tommy, you just kissed Marilyn Monroe," the friend remarked. "What was it like?"

"It was like being swallowed alive," Noonan replied, prompting Maril—who overhead the exchange—to run crying to her dressing room.

"If that had happened to me, I'd say, 'Honey, you should be so lucky!'" Jane asserted.

Bold, brassy, and self-assured, Jane Russell could shrug off the unkind remarks of other people, but Maril was totally vulnerable. Even after achieving stardom, she couldn't shed her insecurities.

I've often thought back to that day in mid-1952 when, donning her headscarf-and-sunglasses disguise, Maril went to see a Jane Russell picture at Grauman's. Little did she know that, less than a year later, on June 26, 1953, the two of them would be dipping their hands and feet in wet cement on the forecourt of that very same theater.

At age twenty-six, Maril's dreams were coming true. She'd never been happier.

* * *

The year 1952 was also a big one for Daddy—not least because he wrote the score for *From Here to Eternity*, a drama based on the bestselling novel by James Jones. It's the story of three soldiers in Hawaii just before the attack on Pearl Harbor. One of the soldiers was played by Frank Sinatra, a longtime friend of my father. Frank and his first wife, Nancy, were often guests in our home before Daddy and Mom divorced in 1948. (Frank and Nancy divorced in 1951; I'd sometimes see Frank's children—Frank Jr., Nancy, and Tina—around Beverly Hills.)

Within the studio system, the musical director was the executive in charge of assigning composers, conductors, and musicians to film projects. Columbia's musical director, Morris Stoloff, chose my father to score *From Here to Eternity*.

From Here to Eternity (1953) with music by Fred Karger

Even without participating in the writing, musical directors always share credit for the film score because of how they'd work closely with the composer to shape it around the movie's storyline. *From Here to Eternity* premiered on July 15, 1953. *Gentlemen Prefer Blondes* did likewise three weeks later, on August 5. Nevertheless, when the score of *From Here to Eternity* was nominated for an Academy Award, only Morris Stoloff's name was mentioned.

Daddy wrote two songs for the film, with lyrics by Robert Wells: "Re-Enlistment Blues" and the title number. Played without lyrics, the latter earned neither of them a screen credit. My father had gone straight to the head of the studio, Harry Cohn, and asked him to include lyrics for the song "From Here to Eternity" in the film. As few as eight bars would have qualified it for a screen credit for Karger and Wells—and *that* would have qualified the song for Oscar contention where Daddy would've been nominated. But Harry Cohn said no. With lyrics, it was released as a 45 rpm single by Capitol Records in

1953, became a big hit, and appeared on the *This 's Sinatra!* album three years later.

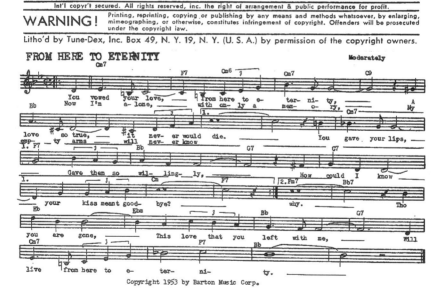

From Here to Eternity (ASCAP) (From the collection of Terry Karger)

In 1953, Maril gave Nana a beautiful gold charm bracelet with a single charm in the shape of a phonograph record. On the front, the record label read, "FROM HERE TO ETERNITY." On the back, she had engraved, "TO ANN, WITH MY DEEPEST LOVE AND FRIENDSHIP, MARILYN."

Charm bracelet gifted to Ann "Nana" Karger by Marilyn Monroe in 1953 (From the collection of Terry Karger)

Maril knew how proud Nana was of Daddy and his accomplishments. More than a present for Nana, that bracelet was also Maril's way of congratulating Daddy for the success of the Capitol Records single *From Here to Eternity*.

* * *

I first met Jane Wyman on Halloween 1952 when Daddy drove me to the actress's beautiful colonial-style Beverly Hills home at 333 South Beverly Glen Boulevard to go trick-or-treating with her children, Maureen and Michael Reagan.

The Holmby Hills house on 333 S. Beverly Glen Blvd. where Jane Wyman and Fred Karger lived during their two marriages

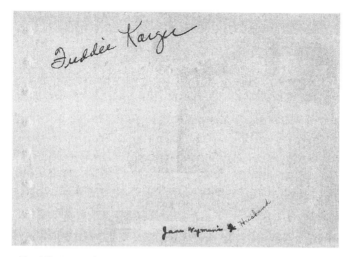

Freddie Karger's signature (From the collection of Terry Karger)

Jane Wyman's signature (From the collection of Terry Karger)

Maureen and I were both eleven; Michael was seven. Jane had been divorced from her third husband, actor Ronald Reagan, for three years, and Ronnie had been married to Nancy Davis since March 1952.

Before Halloween 1952, Maureen and Michael had only met my father once, three weeks prior, even though Daddy and Jane had been dating for months. I myself had never met Jane until, arriving in my

Halloween costume, I was introduced to her, Maureen, and Michael by Daddy.

Jane had all these pictures of girls with great big eyes as you walked in that front door. At the time I saw those paintings, Walter Keane was the credited artist, and we didn't know until years later that it was actually his wife, Margaret Keane, who was responsible for this treasure trove of beautiful artwork. It was a huge wall of pictures of people. All those "eyes" would be staring at you when you walked into Jane's home. I just remember walking in and there were all these "girls" looking at you, but they were paintings done by this well-renowned yet uncredited artist.

All dressed up for the occasion, we three kids were eager to go trick-or-treating, so I was disappointed when Jane said, "Before you go out, I have something to tell you."

This meant sitting down in Jane's den where, I assumed, she was going to lecture us about looking both ways when we crossed the street. Instead, turning to Michael and Maureen, she announced, "Fred is going to be your new father." Then she looked at me and said, "Terry, I'm going to be your new mother."

This was Jane's roundabout way of revealing she and my father were getting married.

I'd long accepted that Maril would never become Daddy's wife, but it hadn't occurred to me he might marry someone else and that I'd have to move from Nana's house into a new home. Sure, I liked Maureen and Michael—and I had always wanted a brother and sister to play with—but now I was forced to accept some major changes in my life.

Jane Wyman on the set of *One More Tomorrow* (May 12, 1946),
Warner Bros. provides Jane with a cake to celebrate her fifth
anniversary as a mother, alongside her fourteen-month-
old son Michael and five-year-old daughter Maureen

Jane Wyman on Mother's Day, May 11, 1947, with her then-husband
Ronald Reagan and their children Michael and Maureen Reagan

That night, trick-or-treating with my future step-siblings, I struggled with the realization that not only would I be seeing less of Nana, Aunt Mary, and my cousins, I'd be living farther away from my mother…and seeing less of Maril.

* * *

At that time, the wedding itself was kept secret from Michael, Maureen, and me. On November 1, 1952, while we visited Ronald Reagan's beautiful Malibu ranch, Daddy and Jane eloped to Santa Barbara where they were married at El Montecito Presbyterian Church.

It was only the next morning, when Jane's housekeeper Carrie gave us rice to throw at the happy couple upon their return, that we put two and two together.

Director Richard Quine was a close friend of Daddy's. As the best man, Richard had the duty of bringing the wedding cake with him on the drive up. After the small ceremony without any reporters present, Jane and Daddy remained in Santa Barbara to have dinner before retiring that Saturday evening at the San Ysidro Hotel.

On Sunday morning, they ate a good breakfast before returning to their home on Beverly Glen.[26]

A few days later, filmland gossip columnist Harrison Carroll began his nationally syndicated newspaper column with a story about the newlyweds:

"The bride, Jane Wyman, is under the care of Dr. Barney Kully. She is suffering from an ulcer on the larynx. It's healing slowly and no surgery will be required."

Theirs had been a whirlwind courtship, conducted after meeting at Columbia Pictures on the set of *Let's Do It Again* (originally titled *Love Song*), a remake of *The Awful Truth*.

Jane Wyman and Freddie Karger at the piano as they rehearse
a song for *Let's Do It Again* (1953) (Weber/Sipa Press)

Jane Wyman in *Let's Do It Again* (1953) (Columbia Pictures)

As filming would wrap in mid-November, Jane told the columnist, "For the first time in seven years, I won't be working at Christmas time."

Asked about a honeymoon, she said, "We probably won't take one. We don't need a honeymoon. We have the rest of our lives to spend together."

They'd actually end up having a belated honeymoon in Las Vegas.

Months after getting married, Jane Wyman and Fred Karger finally enjoy their honeymoon on May 9, 1953, at the Sands in Las Vegas, Nevada (International News/UPI/Corbis)

Meanwhile, Harrison Carroll also noted, "Marilyn Monroe has been promoted to Anne Baxter's former dressing room, the most beautiful on the lot, and, for the first time, will have a studio maid assigned to her."[27]

When the column appeared, Maril had just begun working on *Gentlemen Prefer Blondes* at Twentieth Century-Fox while Jane was doing likewise at Columbia on *Let's Do It Again*. Throughout their first marriage (they would remarry in 1961), my father lived with Jane in her home on Beverly Glen.

November 3, the Monday following Daddy and Jane's wedding, was just another day at the studio; she still had about two more weeks of shooting to complete at Columbia while my father saw even more weeks of work ahead of him in postproduction. Coincidentally, *Let's Do It Again* is the story of an actress (Jane Wyman) married to a composer (Ray Milland). Making their marriage work is difficult and they decide to divorce—before realizing they prefer being together, much as Jane and Daddy would discover a few years later.

Jane Wyman and Fred Karger will leave the set of Columbia's *Let's Do It Again* at the close of work today, Friday, October 31, 1952, for an unannounced destination where they will be married on November 1 (United Press)

Ray Milland congratulates the soon-to-be weds Jane Wyman
and Fred Karger on October 31, 1952 (Photo by Van Pelt)

Jane Wyman with Fred Karger at Columbia Pictures on October 31, 1952

When the two of them arrived at the studio on that Monday morning, they thought their elopement two days earlier was a secret—until the cast and crew shouted, "Surprise!" while a *second* wedding cake was brought onto the set amid shouts demanding speeches from the bride and groom. It was a joyful celebration—as captured by one of Columbia's in-house photographers to help promote the upcoming movie in newspapers across the country.

Newlyweds Fred Karger and Jane Wyman return to Columbia Pictures on Monday, November 3, 1952, to be greeted with a second wedding cake provided by the studio (Associated Press)

Jane Wyman and Fred Karger attend a bridal party on November 3, 1952, tendered them by Columbia Studios where both are currently employed

Jane Wyman and Fred Karger at the piano on November 3, 1952, during their bridal party provided by Columbia Studios (Photo by Nat Dallinger) (King Features Syndicate)

Jack L. Warner greets newlyweds Jane Wyman and Fred Karger on December 15, 1952, at the Louis B. Mayer Screen Producers Guild Milestone Award dinner at the Biltmore Hotel in Los Angeles (Warner Bros. Pictures)

Jane Wyman and Fred Karger with Jeanne Crain and her husband Paul Brickman on December 15, 1952 at the Louis B. Mayer Screen Producers Guild Milestone Award dinner at the Biltmore Hotel in Los Angeles (*The Seattle Times*)

Jane Wyman and her husband Fred Karger are seen
dancing at the Beverly Hills Hotel on December 19, 1952
(Photo by Nat Dallinger) (King Features Syndicate)

A friend of Maril's—gossip columnist Sidney Skolsky—quickly concocted a story about Marilyn Monroe "crashing" a wedding reception for Jane and Daddy at Chasen's restaurant in West Hollywood. Skolsky claimed to be an eyewitness and, even though no such reception ever took place, his account has been repeated in several biographies:

> *The only bitchy thing I ever saw Marilyn do occurred one night at Chasen's. As we approached the checkroom, there was an event taking place in the large private party room ... Marilyn and I were told that the Fred Karger and Jane Wyman wedding party was in the room. (I think it was the second time around for Fred and Jane.) Marilyn said she had to go inside and congratulate Fred. She knew this would burn up Jane Wyman. She boldly crashed the reception and congratulated Fred. As Marilyn and Jane were pretending that they didn't*

know the other was in the same room, the tension in the atmosphere would have been as easy to cut as the wedding cake.[28]

This was pure fabrication. Daddy and Jane never had a wedding reception at Chasen's—not after their 1952 Santa Barbara nuptials or after their 1961 Newport Beach marriage. However, Jane *did* give my father a surprise birthday party at Chasen's on February 13, 1953, which Maril almost attended. But she didn't crash the party. And Sidney Skolsky wasn't there. In the May 1953 issue of *Modern Screen*, Louella Parsons wrote:

What's all this about Marilyn Monroe "crashing" the birthday party Jane Wyman gave for Freddie Karger at Chasen's and "everybody being SOOOOO embarrassed because Freddie used to date Marilyn before he married Jane!" Oh, now—Please! In the first place, a guest at Jane's party in the new private room at Chasen's ran into Marilyn (dining in the café proper) and insisted that the Monroe join the party for a cocktail. Marilyn didn't even know whose party it was until she dropped in for a hot five minutes. As for Janie and Freddie being embarrassed— that's a lot of mush. That Wyman girl whom I love so much is far too good a scout for such nonsense. She asked Marilyn to remain for dinner—but the gal had a couple of escorts waiting for her in the café. Poor Marilyn. No matter what she does she usually gets a blast from some quarter. Getting back to Jane's party, it was one of the few real surprises ever pulled in our town. She kept her plans for a birthday celebration so secret from Freddie that she had the invitations sent out in the names of her good friends Bobbie and Bill Perlberg. When Janie walked in with Freddie, 85 guests were already assembled and his

band broke into the strains of "Happy Birthday to You."
Freddie almost fell over in surprise and delight.[29]

Clearing this up is important to me because Sidney Skolsky, who was supposedly Maril's friend, misrepresented who she was. The "bitchy" thing Skolsky said she did (and claimed to have witnessed with his own eyes) never happened. Maril didn't "boldly crash" any reception with the intent to "burn up" Jane Wyman.

As for Fred and Jane's second wedding on March 11, 1961—I attended the small ceremony in Newport Beach. Uncle John was also an attendee. Daddy and Jane spent the entire weekend there. We didn't drive ninety minutes to a reception at Chasen's, and we never saw Maril or Sidney Skolsky that weekend. He made the whole thing up.

The Marilyn Monroe described by Skolsky is not the Maril I knew. Maril was fun and mischievous, but no way would she deliberately humiliate Jane Wyman in front of her friends. She wasn't cruel, she wasn't vindictive, she wasn't "bitchy," and *that's* the truth.

* * *

Looking back, I now realize I was blessed to live for a while in that beautiful home where I met everyone from actress June Allyson and her singer-actor husband Dick Powell to agent-studio executive Lew Wasserman and gossip columnist Louella Parsons. Through most of my early years, I took Hollywood celebrities for granted. But the night June Allyson came to my room and wanted my opinion on her dress and her freckles—that was *special*.

Jane Wyman and Fred Karger (Photo by Mac Julian)

Jane Wyman and her husband Fred Karger dine at the Cocoanut Grove
on April 10, 1953 (Photo by Nat Dallinger) (King Features Syndicate)

Jane Wyman and Fred Karger sit out a dance at Romanoff's on May 29, 1953 (Photo by Nat Dallinger) (King Features Syndicate)

Fred Karger with his wife Jane Wyman on September 3, 1953, at the premiere of *Island in the Sky* (Culver Pictures)

Fred Karger with Gracie Allen (wife of George Burns), center, and his wife Jane Wyman at the La Rue Restaurant in Hollywood, California on October 30, 1953 (Photo by Nat Dallinger) (King Features Syndicate)

Fred Karger and his wife Jane Wyman are seen together at a dinner party at the Cocoanut Grove in Hollywood on December 11, 1953 (Photo by Nat Dallinger) (King Features Syndicate)

Judy Holliday and dialogue director Gerald Freedman listen to Fred
Karger play *Let's Fall In Love*, a song that was used in Columbia's comedy
It Should Happen to You (1954) (Photo by Lippman) (Columbia Pictures)

Jane Wyman and Fred Karger attend a wedding reception on
March 19, 1954, in Beverly Hills, California. Hollywood friends
noted that the couple seemed happy again after a series of marital
rifts. (Photo by Nat Dallinger) (Kings Features Syndicate)

**Jane Wyman and Fred Karger attend a first showing in Hollywood
of her newest film *Magnificent Obsession* on April 30, 1954
(Photo by Nat Dallinger) (King Features Syndicate)**

**Jane Wyman and Fred Karger are among the audience at the
Ice Follies in Hollywood, California, on October 22, 1954
(Photo by Nat Dallinger) (King Features Syndicate)**

Fred Karger, Janet Leigh, Betty Garrett, and Bob Fosse rehearse a
song for Columbia's musical version of *My Sister Eileen* (1955)

After Daddy and I moved in with Jane, Maureen, and Michael, I
had plenty of fun with my new siblings—going swimming and bicycle riding and playing hide-and-seek in Jane's gigantic house. I also
remember playing gin rummy with Michael every summer morning.

Michael is justly proud of his mother, Jane Wyman. He recalled
how Jane prepared for her Oscar-winning role as Belinda McDonald,
a deaf-mute rape victim, in *Johnny Belinda* (1948).

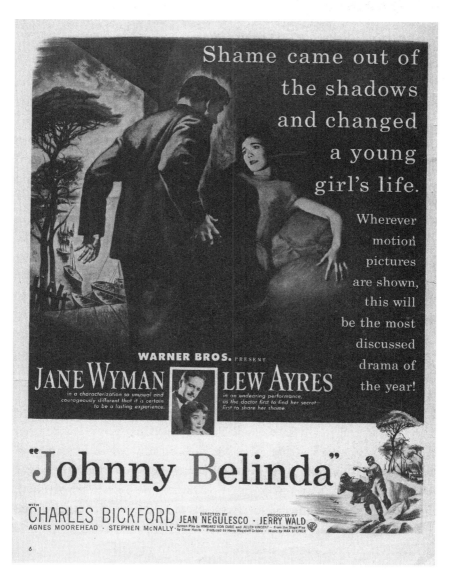

Johnny Belinda (1948), the motion picture where Jane
Wyman won her Academy Award for Best Actress

"Mom stayed in character," Michael said. "She learned sign language and also taught my sister, who was four years older than me. They used to walk around signing to each other. I'd think to myself, 'What the hell have I done?' because nobody was talking to me. Everybody was signing! But she lived in character when making that movie.

"She won the Academy Award for Best Actress. In those days, the Academy would do an oil painting of the Best Actor and Best Actress in character. So they did one of her and it's something like twenty-four by thirty-six, weighing almost a hundred pounds. My mom used to say to me, as older actresses do, 'When I die, what do you want?' I said, 'Mom, just give me Belinda!' So she gave me the Belinda painting, which I have hanging in my house, a little portrait of her in character.

"Mom was very smart. She got a release from Warners to be able to do movies like *Johnny Belinda* because she thought she was being pigeonholed in the industry as the comedic song-and-dance girl. She was known around the set as 'One-Take Wyman.' When she came to work, she was a one-taker. You didn't want to be working with her and be on your third take in the scene. Mom was one of the few people who saved her money, and she ended up firing her business manager, taking over all of her funds herself.

"When she did *Jane Wyman Presents the Fireside Theatre* (1955–1958), they gave her a million-dollar signing bonus, which was huge. She took it and put it into a self-liquidating trust fund. I asked her one time why she did that. She said, 'I'll be too old to be this part. Too young to be that part. I don't want to be a part just to make a living, and it may be a terrible part. I want to be able to get through that era.' So that's what she survived on when she wasn't acting—that self-liquidating trust fund. And when she died, she gave $100,000 to her church, Sacred Heart. She took control of herself."

HOPE ENTERPRISES, INC.

9538 Brighton Way • Beverly Hills, California • CRestview 1-7231

January 29, 1960

Miss Jane Wyman
c/o MCA Artists,Ltd.
    att: Mr. Arthur Parks
9370 Santa Monica Boulevard
Beverly Hills, California

Dear Miss Wyman:

Hope Enterprises, Inc. has entered into an agreement with the National Broadcasting Co.,Inc. for the repeat use of the BOB HOPE DAYTIME RADIO PROGRAMS. The original strip programs will be edited into ten 3-minute spots, not more than five of which will contain your recorded performance, and will be reused as a part of the NBC network program "Monitor" which program is on the air each weekend. This reuse is being sponsored by "Fritos".

You originally appeared in two strip programs and it is now our desire to reuse these programs over two separate weekends within the next 13-week period.

Your signature below will confirm our agreement as follows:

You agree that as full compensation for the rights granted hereunder you will accept the sum of $168 per strip in which your recorded performance appears; you will not be required to render any personal services in connection with this reuse.

The rights that you grant to Hope Enterprises, Inc. shall be limited to the use of recorded performances for one network broadcast of each strip as described above, and only such supplementary broadcasts as may be required by the NBC Radio Network.

Hope Enterprises, Inc. shall have no option to renew this agreement with you without your and AFTRA's further consent.

If the foregoing meets with your approval, please indicate your acceptance in the space provided below and return one copy of this letter to us as soon as possible.

Very truly yours,

HOPE ENTERPRISES, INC.

AGREED TO AND ACCEPTED:

Jane Wyman

By _James V. Saphier_

**Jane Wyman's contract with Hope Enterprises, Inc. on January 29, 1960
(From the collection of Terry Karger)**

* * *

Jane and Daddy spoiled me a bit while I was living in her house. One birthday, they gave me a Rolex watch with different-colored leather straps. I really wanted the watch with the gold band, and I said so. At the next holiday, they gave it to me. One Christmas, Jane and my dad gave me a brand-new bicycle, and I cried because I wanted one like Maureen's, even though her bike was five years old. I get embarrassed now when I think about my behavior. It wasn't until I began earning my own money that I learned to appreciate the value of things.

When we got older, Michael, Maureen, and I enrolled in swim classes to become junior lifeguards. I was already a swimmer and we passed the test. To this day, I don't know that we ever got our certificates. We were so proud it didn't matter.

Every other Saturday, Ronald Reagan would pick up Maureen, Michael, and me in his Ford station wagon. He was doing TV commercials for Ford at that time, and we'd visit his ranch for the weekend to hike, ride horses, and have a great time.

Meanwhile, my cousin Johnny Warren came to live with us at Jane's home because his parents were in the middle of a marital crisis. Ronnie would take Johnny along with the rest of us to the ranch on weekends. He taught Johnny and Michael how to ride horses and shoot a rifle. Believe it or not, I even had my own goat on the ranch.

Nancy Reagan would often come along, bringing little Patti, who was an infant then, a baby in the crib. The Reagan station wagon could get a bit crowded, but we didn't mind. Ronnie taught us all kinds of games to play and songs to sing to make the drive seem shorter. We'd sing patriotic songs like the "Marines' Hymn" and silly songs like "Ninety-Nine Bottles of Beer on the Wall."

Johnny recalled, "Ronnie would say, 'Johnny, you harmonize!' He was like a dad to me. Ronnie was very down-to-earth. Terry and I got to know him, and he was a very loving, fatherly figure to me at a time when I needed that kind of attention."

Ronald Reagan was a caring and lovable man—athletic, charming, and understanding. We got to know him and Nancy very well. Johnny and I were vaguely aware that Ronnie was an actor, but that didn't mean much to us because most of the adults in our lives were in show business. What impressed us about Ronnie and Nancy was their kindness and all the fun we had at the ranch or at the Reagan home in Pacific Palisades.

Ronald Reagan, Bob Cummings, and Art Linkletter host
the live ninety-minute, coast-to-coast television broadcast
for Disneyland's opening on July 17, 1955

"I understand more now than I did back then when I was a child,"
Michael recalled. "I used to harass my father because he was one of the
three people who had opened up Disneyland back in 1955 with Art
Linkletter and Bob Cummings. I said to my dad, 'Was there any time
during that day when you thought to yourself, "I should have brought
the kids!"' And he said, 'I never thought of it.' Today I understand it
was work to him and not a day to bring children, so he saw it as a job.
What I realize now is that the best time I ever had with my dad was
going to the ranch *before* he got into politics.

"Dad never took us to a baseball game or a football game. The
only reason we never went was because he knew he couldn't just take
me to a game, sit down, and enjoy it without a horde of people who
wanted their picture taken with him or wanted his autograph. We'd
never really see the game. We just didn't go. So instead, we would
spend our time at the ranch riding horses and chopping wood because
he felt comfortable there. At the end of the day, we would always be
swimming in the pool. You could go out there and just be family."

Jane Wyman's daughter Maureen Reagan attends her first Hollywood premiere on September 5, 1951 (*The Blue Veil*) at the age of ten, seeing her mother on screen for the first time (Associated Press)

Johnny reminisced, "In 1952, I once went with Jane and Freddie to see her latest movie, *The Story of Will Rogers*, at the Carthay Circle Theatre. We were with Michael, Maureen, and Terry. So we all went to the movies in Beverly Hills to see Jane's latest film, and no one knew she was there. I loved the film and I told Jane, 'I really liked your film. I thought it was beautiful.' Terry didn't say anything. When we were walking back to the car, Maureen was crying and she said, 'I didn't like you in that film, Mom.' I didn't agree. Jane played a terrific young lady and I thought, 'Wow, this is great!'

"I lived in Jane's home during the summer of 1953. I often went there during the weekends, and Michael sometimes came to our home in the San Fernando Valley. I bunked with Michael—we had one bedroom while Maureen and Terry had theirs. We got to know each other pretty well. Terry and I loved Maureen—we called her Mermie. Maureen was a sweetheart.

"Mike and I made models and built different things. Michael was so funny. He'd get upset sometimes and he'd say, 'I don't know and I don't care! It'll work out just fine!' His birthday was on March 18 and mine was on March 22, so they combined the two birthdays for one big party. We invited all our friends and it was so much fun."

Johnny also recalls, just months before, attending Maureen's birthday party at the Music Corporation of America's Beverly Hills headquarters on January 4, 1953, as well as Jane Wyman's own home-based birthday party the very next day:

"I was about twelve years old, and Freddie invited my family over for Jane's party. Maureen and Michael were there along with Terry and my sister Jacqui. As usual with our parties, all of the kids were expected to get up to perform—usually a song or a skit. Sometimes we'd just improvise.

"At one point, the doorbell rang and, when Michael opened the front door, there was Marilyn Monroe. 'Hi, how are you guys?' she asked while Michael stared before eventually saying, 'Good. Come on in!' So Marilyn joined the party—and provided some of the evening's entertainment, performing 'Diamonds Are a Girl's Best Friend.' It was an amazing night."

Eleven years old, I wasn't versed in adult issues involving wives, husbands, and ex-lovers, so Maril showing up at Jane Wyman's birthday party seemed perfectly normal. Daddy had invited his ex-girlfriend there because of how close she was to Nana—and, as Michael said, his mother just wasn't the jealous type. As Louella Parsons once observed, "that Wyman girl" was "a good scout," and a potentially awkward situation therefore worked out just fine. Two years later, in 1955, Jane, Maureen, Johnny, and Johnny's mother Rita Warren received the rite of confirmation at Saint Victor Catholic Church in West Hollywood.

* * *

When Jane was home, we ate formal dinners in the dining room. We were expected to dress up and remember our manners. Jane often had a riding crop at her side. I know the phrase "riding crop" may sound like something out of *Mommie Dearest*, but it wasn't like that at all. Jane was a very kind and loving lady but a strict disciplinarian. She didn't use the riding crop to inflict pain but to get our attention. If one of us kids started misbehaving, we'd hear the *thwip!* of that riding crop against the table and we instantly snapped to.

Michael recalls that his dad, Ronald Reagan, was "the push-over in the family." The two women he married, Jane Wyman and Nancy Davis, were the disciplinarians. "I think the only people Dad disciplined," Michael said, "were Muammar Gaddafi and Mikhail Gorbachev. He never disciplined anybody in the family. If I did something wrong, I always wanted to tell Dad about it, not Mom or Nancy."

Michael, Maureen, my cousin Johnny, and I had a lot of fun together, living on Beverly Glen with Jane Wyman and my dad. Admittedly, a lot of that fun was mischief. Jane had a lamp in her breakfast room made from an antique coffee grinder. Once, when there were no grown-ups around, we put our hamburgers into the coffee grinder and turned the crank to see what happened. It made quite a mess of the grinder, and Jane made us clean it up.

Another time, when Daddy and Jane were away, the four of us had a food fight. Food was everywhere—on the walls, the ceiling, the windows, everywhere. It was epic! Carrie, the cook, came in and shrieked. When Daddy and Jane returned home, the food *really* hit the fan.

Carrie was more a member of the family than an employee. When she died, Jane, Maureen, and Michael attended her funeral in Jane's Rolls-Royce.

The home of Academy Award–winning actress Jane Wyman was a popular attraction for those "homes of the stars" bus tours. This was all new to my cousin Johnny and me, but Michael and Maureen had been living in the Hollywood fishbowl for years. Once, when we were in the front yard and a tour bus was coming up Beverly Glen,

Maureen told us to duck behind the bushes. As the bus crawled past Jane's house, we all screamed bloody murder. The bus sped away.

Maureen and I were the same age but opposite personalities. Maureen enjoyed the spotlight and planned to be famous, like her parents. I didn't care about fame. That's why I went into teaching while Maureen went into acting (she appeared in *Kissin' Cousins* with Elvis Presley and on several TV shows, including *The Partridge Family*, *Marcus Welby, M.D.*, and *The Love Boat*).

On March 2, 1974, Maureen Reagan and her mother Jane Wyman are studying their scripts for *The Partridge Family* and *Owen Marshall, Counselor at Law*, respectively (Associated Press)

Later, she turned to politics.

Michael once told me Maureen was jealous of me. He said she didn't like it when I came to live with them because I took attention away from her. Whenever Maureen and I were out walking, she made me walk a hundred feet in front of her. It baffled me, because Maureen was quite attractive, like her mother. I don't know why she was insecure, but I imagine it had something to do with being the child of famous people.

"Maureen was terrific," Michael remembered. "I think the world misses her right now. Politically, she was strong-willed and was the only daughter until Terry came around. Terry's easygoing and soft-spoken and was like a lot of kids from Hollywood in those days. Terry had a better feeling for Maureen than Maureen probably had for Terry because there was a jealousy to a certain extent. There's another girl in the room. In Hollywood, you don't spend an inordinate amount of time with your parents, and the only person Maureen wanted to share that with was me.

"In that era, in Hollywood, all of us were in boarding schools. Maureen was at Chadwick in Palos Verdes Peninsula when she was old enough to go to school. When I was about six years old, I also went to Chadwick. Maureen was like my big sister/mother, looking over me at Chadwick. Depending on what school we were at, I would come home on a Friday or Saturday. We would go to the Brown Derby or we would go to Chasen's for dinner.

"So the time you got to spend with your parents was really a kind of special time. Now with Terry, you're bringing another child into the room who's now there to spend your time. Maureen was a little tougher to share our mother. It was what it was. I had two sisters and there you go …

"For my twenty-first birthday, my mom says, 'I wanna throw a party for ya.' 'Okay.' She doesn't allow me to invite any of my friends, but she invited hers. One of them was Cesar Romero, who played the Joker in *Batman* (1966). It ends up being on the second floor at Chasen's on Beverly Boulevard.

"The coup de grâce was she called me on the phone saying, 'You're going to love your date.' I said 'What?' 'I know this wonderful girl.' 'Mom, I might have someone I'd like to invite.' 'I've already set it up. You're taking her.' 'Who's her?' So I took Ricardo Montalbán's daughter to my twenty-first birthday party. I never saw this young girl again in my life. My mom said, 'If you want your friends, *you* throw the party.' Ricardo Montalbán's wife has twin sisters. One was Sally Foster, who was my godmother."

Sally was Loretta Young's sister. Loretta had won the Best Actress Academy Award for *The Farmer's Daughter* (1947), one year before Jane won her Best Actress Oscar for *Johnny Belinda* (1948). At the end of Jane's life, she and Loretta became very close. They both lived in Rancho Mirage near Palm Springs. They were strong Catholics and that made them even closer. Years later at Jane's funeral, Michael introduced me to Jane's caretaker, who had previously been with Loretta Young. Loretta died before Jane.

Looking back, I'm amazed at the privileges I enjoyed as a child, privileges I took for granted. I mean, what are the odds I'd become personally acquainted with not only innumerable celebrities and a future president but also the most iconic actress of the twentieth century? It was a special time.

5: MAUREEN WAVES HER MAGICAL POLITICAL WAND

My stepsister Maureen ran unsuccessfully for the United States Senate in 1982, and she and Michael worked tirelessly in Ronald Reagan's presidential campaigns. Michael remembered, "Before Mom became the highest-paid TV actress in Hollywood with *Falcon Crest*, my dad made his announcement for the presidency at the Hilton Hotel ballroom in New York City for the 1980 campaign. My dad's run for the presidency, to him, was like getting an Eagle Scout badge. That's probably the way he looked at it. He was an easygoing guy who did what he wanted and did what he thought to get by and tried to communicate that to other people.

"Maureen was very politically active. She was one of the first to say back in 1962, 'Our father someday is going to be president of the United States,' and he hadn't even done 'A Time for Choosing' speech, which wasn't to be delivered for another two years. She also had a sense of humor. Maureen, my wife Colleen, and I were on a midnight flight to fly in because that was the only thing the campaign could put us on. When we got off the plane, nobody was there to meet us. So we got a cab, went to a hotel, and our room wasn't ready.

"Maureen said to me and Colleen, 'Why don't we just go on a tour of New York?' at which point one of the operatives showed up at the hotel and asked, 'Is everything okay?' Maureen would have one of these staring looks like 'Why do you ask?' 'I want to know how you're doing.' 'You'll know tonight.' 'How will I know?' She says, 'I brought two sets of heels with me for tonight's announcement. One foot makes me taller than your candidate. The other makes me shorter.' So that was Merm. You'll never see that side of Terry.

"What can you do to become bigger when you have such an iconic parent? Maureen dealt with that and said, 'The campaign is not treating us the way the campaign should.' Remember, my father was the first president to be nominated and elected who had been divorced. So you have a situation where the campaign is very worried about having Michael and Maureen campaigning for their father, and there are some within the family concerned that people were going to be running around saying that Ronald Reagan was divorced.

"I remember Maureen was invited to meet with Nancy, and Nancy wanted to talk to her about that situation. And Nancy said to Maureen, 'We're having some kickback where people are going to be reminded that there are those on the campaign trail who are not aware that your father in fact was married before. And you need not remind people of that. What do you have to say to that?'

"Maureen says, 'You're probably hearing from people who didn't know that my father had been married before, but there aren't any people on the campaign trail who are never getting a divorce.' That's how Maureen sometimes gets you. She was more in-your-face. Your jaw hits the floor.

"When our father was running for president, she was a big Equal Rights Amendment supporter. The campaign went to her and said, 'Maureen, you know your father is not an advocate for the Equal Rights Amendment. What can we do to have you stop campaigning for that and instead just campaign for your father?' Dad's in the room with me, my sister, and the campaign staff. My sister looks at the campaign staff away from her father and says, 'Well, if you can get your candidate to guarantee me that if he's elected president of the United States, his first appointment to the Supreme Court will be a woman, I will stop campaigning for the Equal Rights Amendment.' Dad said, 'Deal.'

"So my sister and my father made a deal that day. My sister quit campaigning for the Equal Rights Amendment. However, at the convention back in Detroit, my sister has this huge button which says E-R-A on it. And the staff goes, 'Oh my God, she has gone back on her word! Here she is advocating the Equal Rights Amendment!' But if you got up really close to the button, what it said was 'Elect Reagan Anyway.' So our father goes on to win the presidency of the United States, and now we know how Sandra Day O'Connor got nominated to the Supreme Court of our land!"

6: MUSICAL HOUR

SOME OF MY MOST cherished memories of Maril revolve around the Sunday night gatherings we called Musical Hour. This was a family talent show and, because Maril was part of our family, she often joined in—along with my cousins when they stayed for the weekend.

The party always began with dinner, and we rarely had fewer than a dozen or so people. Following a splendid meal, we'd then move to the living room where we had a piano and space to perform by the fireplace.

Everybody participated at these weekly musical recitals—adults and children, professionals and amateurs—and we all had to come up with an impromptu song or dance on the spot. Because our audience consisted of relatives, we could always count on plenty of support and enthusiasm. In addition to all the amateur talent in our family, we had two retired vaudevillians: Nana and her sister Effie. And, of course, we had Daddy at the piano with his lovely protégé, Marilyn Monroe.

My cousin Anne and I both took ballet lessons from a prestigious Russian teacher, but Anne was a better dancer. While she loved to dance, I preferred to sing.

Every singer needs a microphone, and mine was an empty tennis ball can over a broom handle. I'd try to remember everything Daddy taught me about singing (I had the same vocal coach as Ms. Monroe, after all). For a few minutes, I could shed my inhibitions and perform like a star; those Sunday night Musical Hours helped me overcome my shyness.

In my mind, I can still hear Nana singing an old sentimental ballad from the vaudeville stage called "When You Were Sweet Sixteen":

Come to me, or my dream of love is o'er.
I love you as I loved you
When you were sweet—
When you were sweet sixteen.

Nana's brother, my great-uncle John Conley, sometimes sang a bouncy tune called "Big Chief So-and-So," followed by my great-aunt Effie singing and dancing to "I Learned More from Willie That Night Than I Learned from a Whole Year at School." She'd finish her dance routine with a can-can and daring flash of frilly red panties. I didn't know what the lyrics meant at the time but, looking back, they were slightly risqué.

Ben and Anne's stepfather, Major Walter Short, was no Sinatra, but he could perform a pleasing rendition of "Melancholy Baby." (As Maril says in *Some Like It Hot*, "All they have to do is play eight bars of 'Come to Me My Melancholy Baby' and my spine turns to custard and I get goose pimply all over!")

The showstopper, of course, was Maril—accompanied by Daddy. Performing "Diamonds Are a Girl's Best Friend" by the fireplace in Nana's living room with the same energy as in *Gentlemen Prefer Blondes*, she brought the house down. Without a stage, lavish costume, or dozens of backup dancers, she still danced and sang as if she did.

Maril taught my cousin Anne and me to sing that number with all the gestures and dance moves. I have a real vivid memory of watching Anne perform it while descending the stairs in Nana's two-story house. She was so much fun to be with. Anne would pass away too soon, in 1997, and I still miss her very much.

* * *

My cousin Johnny, who briefly lived with us at Jane Wyman's house, recalls how Jane "gave me a Brush Company tape recorder. It used magnetic-coated paper tape on seven-and-a-half-inch reels. I used it to experiment with sound recording and I also took it to the family Musical Hours. Marilyn used the amplifier on the tape recorder as a PA system when she performed 'Diamonds Are a Girl's Best Friend' at Jane's birthday party in January 1953.

"Wouldn't it be fun to hear Marilyn again, singing that song with Freddie at the piano? She wouldn't just sing it—she had it choreographed and she would strut it. We loved that. There were family talent nights every Thanksgiving, and Marilyn would be there because she was family, too. We'd all perform and I'd record each performance; I wish I still had those tapes, but they are long gone."

"I first met Marilyn when I was about fourteen," adds Johnny's sister, Jacqui. "She was so friendly and uninhibited—just a lovely, fun gal. Freddie would bring her over to the Harper house and we'd all perform. Coming from a theatrical family, we were expected to put on a show. And, although I was shy and so embarrassed, I'd sing and dance, too."

By 1953, Maril had begun sipping her favorite pink champagne, Dom Pérignon, at social gatherings (a compromise of the Christian Science principles her Aunt Ana Lower had taught her). At one of our Sunday night gatherings, she was on her second or third glass when, getting up to sing, she tripped over Effie and staggered toward the piano.

"Sorry, Aunt Effie!" Maril giggled before, leaning against the baby grand piano played by Daddy, she delivered a steamy, slightly tipsy rendition of the great 1922 George Gershwin/Buddy DeSylva composition "Do It Again." She acted out the song as much as she sang it, providing a sensuous syncopation that I'm sure the songwriters never envisioned.

When she finished, the room was silent. Applause wasn't just customary, it was practically mandatory, so Maril's eyes widened with panic as she stared at the audience. Then the room erupted in applause. Completely mesmerized, everyone rose to give her a standing ovation and shower her with hugs. Even at our little Sunday night family musicals, Maril had that kind of impact as a performer.

"It was really beautiful to watch Marilyn sing that number," recalls my cousin Jacqui. " 'Do It Again' and 'Diamonds Are a Girl's Best Friend' were the two songs she knew by heart."

As Maril herself once said:

> *I don't try to kid myself about it. I do think though that if you can put some feeling into a song, you don't need a spectacular voice. I try my best to feel what I'm singing by painting word images. For instance, if a song is about loneliness, I think of a stretch of desolate beach with a solitary figure staring out to sea. I do the same thing with a love ballad, putting myself in the place of the girl and forcing myself to feel her problem is my problem and her happiness is my happiness ... I try to put my whole body into a song. A twist of the head, a clasp of the hands, a slight shiver may convey more feeling in a song sometimes than all of the lyrics.*[30]

Maril's self-assessment was characteristically humble. She was an *amazing* vocalist with an exceptional ability to feel and express the meaning of a song. Recognizing her talent, my father helped her develop and refine it while trying to build her confidence. From the very beginning, he knew she had the makings of a star.

* * *

Once, when I was with my cousin Johnny Warren, Maril gave me a 16 mm movie projector plus several films starring Abbott and Costello. Never a fan of that comedy duo, I didn't really need a projector. But, looking into Johnny's eyes, I could tell *he* did. After all, Johnny was the film buff.

"I doubt that I'll use a projector very much, but I think Johnny would love to have one—wouldn't you, Johnny?"

"You bet!" he exclaimed.

"Maril, is it okay if I give this to Johnny?"

"Sure, go ahead."

Johnny was thrilled. Years later, he said that projector—along with a movie camera and sound equipment he acquired—fired up his youthful desire to work in the motion picture industry. My cousins and I benefitted from Maril's generous nature in more ways than I can count.

* * *

Because Maril had grown up without a father and with an unavailable mother, she was acutely aware of the blessing my cousins and I enjoyed thanks to parents who were involved in our lives. Yes, my parents were divorced, but they and my cousins' parents still cared about us. We knew we were loved; Maril never had that, which is why, if she saw us being ungrateful, disobedient, or disrespectful to our parents, she felt it in a personal way.

It truly hurt her. More than once, she took me aside and gently but earnestly suggested I listen to my father because he wanted what was best for me. She'd also tell me to apologize to my mother for being rude. Accustomed to Maril usually being more of a sister than an authority figure in my life, I was surprised. Yet, looking back, I realize these admonitions stemmed from her conviction that I should be grateful for the parents I had—and she never had.

I could confide things in Maril that I couldn't tell my parents. If I complained about Mom studying law or Daddy not giving me enough attention, Maril would listen to my tale of woe and then tell me a story from her own childhood. By putting my problems in perspective, she helped me to understand instead of feeling sorry for myself.

When I was in my teens, we talked about makeup and men. Maril told me how great it was to know people like Bob Mitchum and Marlon Brando. She said men were easier to talk with than most women her age. Nana was like a mother to her and she could tell her anything, but younger women were often judgmental and cruel.

When Maril was on a movie set, she'd sometimes overhear women talking about her behind her back. She told me she didn't have many female friends besides Nana, Mom, and Aunt Mary, so going to a man for support often made things easier. After all, they just loved the pleasure of her company and were too polite to judge.

"I like talking to you, T.K.," she once told me. "You're like a kid sister."

Being an only child, I loved hearing her say that. I couldn't have asked for a sweeter, kinder big sister than Maril. She said she knew I would never betray her. I told her of course I wouldn't. I never judged her.

When Maril was at our house, she dressed casually and wore no makeup. But then, when she was getting ready to go out, I'd watch her apply makeup and put on her "Marilyn Monroe" face while explaining what she was doing with lipstick or eye shadow. I couldn't help noticing how flawless her skin was and wanted to ask what she did to keep it so beautiful, but I never had the nerve.

Maril also showed me how she posed when attending the Blue Book Modeling Agency. Using the living room as a theater, she'd stand very focused in front of me, repeat a few moves she'd learned, and laugh that beautiful laugh of hers. I'll never forget that laugh. I loved it.

* * *

I have to tell you about the Russell Roadhouse ...

Jack Russell—or John L. Russell, as he was listed in movie and television credits—was an Oscar-nominated cinematographer for Alfred Hitchcock's *Psycho* (1960). The cinematographer directs the lighting and camera crews for a TV show or motion picture. Jack also worked on Orson Welles's *Macbeth* (1948) and countless television series, including *Alfred Hitchcock Presents*, *Death Valley Days*, *Run for Your Life*, and *General Electric Theater*.

Back when land in the San Fernando Valley was relatively cheap, Jack bought a three-acre farm in Studio City and built a ranch-style home there. The house was constructed of knotty pine, the living room had a chandelier made from an old wagon wheel, a bearskin rug was spread on the floor, and there were fancy attractions for kids to enjoy: a swimming pool, a small roller coaster, an archery range, and bike paths that meandered all around the place. Much of the furniture was handmade by Jack himself.

Living there with his wife Vi and their sons, Michael and John, Jack called his home the Russell Roadhouse and hosted some amazing events there: Easter egg hunts, Fourth of July celebrations with dazzling fireworks displays, and the best New Year's Eve parties on the planet. Daddy brought Maril to a number of those gatherings, even after their romance ended. Jack had an upright piano in the dining hall, Daddy would play the old standards, and everybody would gather around to sing. Given all the showbiz guests, there was never a shortage of performing talent.

Jack himself was famed for his rendition of "On the Road to Mandalay," Nana and Effie performed some of their old routines, and when Maril was there, it didn't take much coaxing from Daddy to get her to sing a number from her latest film. Likewise, everyone enjoyed Nana's famed Hollywood hospitality at her house on Harper Avenue. Jack's son, Mike Russell, recalls meeting Maril there as a seven-year-old:

"When Marilyn arrived, people made a big fuss over this starlet. And everybody always made a big fuss over that charismatic guy Fred Karger. I'm not gay, but anybody would think Fred was handsome. He was a lady-killer as well as a very nice man. Anyway, Marilyn sat down and started gushing over me, saying things like, 'Aren't you *adorable*.' She even had me sit on her lap. At first I was kind of embarrassed, but hugging and giving me plenty of attention soon changed my mind. In retrospect, I wish I hadn't been so innocent."

Another frequent guest at the Russell Roadhouse was Russ Tamblyn, the sixteen-year-old actor and dancer who'd soon be Oscar-nominated for his performance as Norman Page in *Peyton Place* (1957), play the title role in *Tom Thumb* (1958), and star as Riff, the leader of the Jets, in *West Side Story* (1961). As a boy, Rusty dreamed of becoming a circus acrobat. So, in addition to singing and dancing, he'd also wow us with his juggling and tumbling.

Now almost seventeen and already a motion picture veteran, Rusty was dating my fifteen-year-old cousin Jacqui. "He was my puppy love," she recalls. "He lived in North Hollywood, I lived in Sherman Oaks, and, shooting the Korean War film *Retreat, Hell!* (1952) he gave me a bayonet from one of the rifles they'd used. We had a lot of fun and used to go dancing at the Palladium in Hollywood. He was such a terrific dancer, people called him 'Tumbling Tamblyn of North Hollywood.' We dated for a year, and Rusty was the first man I fell in love with."

"I certainly remember Jacqui very well," says Russ Tamblyn. "She lived above Ventura Boulevard in Sherman Oaks and had a beautiful house and a great family. We went together in high school and she was just a wonderfully sweet girl. We danced and had a really great time.

"While dating Jacqui, I was in one of Marilyn Monroe's first pictures, *As Young as You Feel*, with Monty Woolley, Albert Dekker, and Constance Bennett. Marilyn had a small part as a secretary and was only in a few scenes. When I met her on the set, I thought, 'Boy, is she beautiful!' Running her fingers through my hair, she said, 'You have such beautiful curly hair.' Usually, I wouldn't let anybody do that, but she was so pretty I couldn't help but *let* her do that!"

We had so many priceless memories at the Russell Roadhouse. Unfortunately, however, Jack Russell's wonderful home and grounds were demolished and paved over in the late 1950s when the 101 Freeway came through the San Fernando Valley.

7: MARIL AND JOE

ON THE SURFACE, MY father Fred Karger had little in common with Maril's next love, New York Yankees baseball legend Joe DiMaggio. However, there were some interesting parallels between the two men.

Both were considerably older than Maril—Daddy by eleven years, Joe by a dozen. Both were impeccably dressed, soft-spoken, and elegantly mannered; both were devoted to their large, close-knit families; and both radiated a refinement and fatherliness, which Maril found very attractive in a man. She later told Nana one thing she liked about Joe was the touch of gray hair at his temples.

Joe DiMaggio and Marilyn Monroe by John Vachon in 1953

Starting in 1952 and continuing through 1953, Maril dated the "Yankee Clipper" while, having met playwright Arthur Miller on the set of *As Young as You Feel* (1951), she maintained a long-distance friendship with him, too—conducted mostly via letters and phone calls.

In June of '53, Maril boarded a train bound for Canada to begin filming her second CinemaScope picture, *River of No Return*, costarring Robert Mitchum, directed by Otto Preminger. Along for the ride was her acting coach Natasha Lytess—leading to no end of trouble on the set. During filming, Natasha repeatedly took Maril aside to countermand the direction Preminger had given her. When Preminger banned Natasha from the set, Maril telephoned Fox studio chief Darryl Zanuck and demanded she be reinstated. Prevailed upon by Zanuck, Preminger backed off—but then took out his frustration on the superstar leading lady.

Having worked alongside Maril's first husband, Jim Dougherty, when they were machine operators at Lockheed Aircraft, Mitchum had known Maril as unknown Norma Jeane Dougherty. Back then, according to him, she was "very shy, very pleasant, very sweet, but she was not too comfortable around people… She was convinced she was not terribly pretty or sexy."

Now that she was Marilyn Monroe, how did she regard herself?

"She thought that this whole lark of being a sex goddess or a glamour queen was just that. She would play it if that's what they wanted. And, as a matter of fact, she burlesqued it, really. Because she thought the whole thing was very, very funny… She thought the whole thing was a lie because that was *not* her.

"She was a very special girl, and she had an enormous feeling for people. When we came back from Canada, we were doing close-up work: the stuff we were doing on the raft in the white water. There was a fellow in the tank blasting us with a high-pressure fire hose, and she suddenly looked over at him and started almost whimpering. I said, 'What is it?' She said, 'Look at him. He's freezing. He's turning blue. That man is suffering.' And she wouldn't work until they replaced him with somebody who was warmer."[31]

Maril returned with stories of her adventures in Canada. She told Nana and me about preparing to shoot a scene on the river. Rehearsing while wearing rubber hip boots to keep her costume from getting wet, she slipped, fell into the river, and the hip boots filled with water. As she was sinking, Robert Mitchum jumped into the water and saved her from drowning, but her ankle was sprained and her costume was soaked.

She also told me about a scene she shot aboard the raft during an Indian attack. An actor portraying an Indian "got a little too frisky" and clearly enjoyed running his hands all over her during the struggle. "I had to watch out for him," she said, laughing.

Filming on *River of No Return* ended in late September (with a few days of retakes in November and December). Lionel Newman and Ken Darby wrote several beautiful songs that Maril sang in the film, including the sweet and childlike "Down in the Meadow" and bluesy "I'm Gonna File My Claim." Nevertheless, my favorite is the title song, which she embellished with a wistful, sentimental touch that brings tears to my eyes and makes me wonder: Did Daddy teach her how to convey the emotion throbbing in her voice or did Maril find that within her own soul?

* * *

In January 1953, Maril moved into Apartment 3 at 882 North Doheny Drive, a one-bedroom, single-bathroom second-floor apartment that Jane Russell helped her decorate. She lived there for a year until her marriage to Joe and, since my cousin Jacqui worked nearby in the registrar's office at UCLA, she occasionally visited Maril.

"Marilyn was like family," Jacqui says. "She'd go in the bathroom for half an hour and put on her pretty makeup. I always think of her as just the natural Marilyn, not the big star. At her Doheny apartment she'd give me clothes and little shirts—things she no longer needed.

She loved to open her closet and give people things. She was just really cute.

"When my UCLA coworkers found out I knew her, they'd say, 'You have a blouse that belonged to Marilyn Monroe? You have a skirt she wore?' I'd say, 'Sure, would you like to have it?' Giving them something of Marilyn's meant so much to those people, but for me it was just normal.

"The Maril we knew was so unlike her image. When I'd visit her apartment, she'd lounge on the couch; so cute, so relaxed. She was also funny, which is why we'd laugh all the time. She never put on any false front around our family. She could be herself. The Maril we knew was so innocent and joyful."

Maril's most entertaining TV appearance was on *The Jack Benny Program*. Airing live from LA's Shrine Auditorium on Sunday, September 13, 1953, the opening show of Jack's fourth season was one of the most-watched small-screen events of the year. I was at Nana's house that day when Maril dropped by to tell us she'd been rehearsing all week and would be playing "Marilyn Monroe," based on a very funny script penned by Jack Benny's writers.

That evening, Nana, Aunt Mary, my cousins, and I watched some of Maril's best work as a comedienne. Being live TV, it was like a stage performance, executed in one continuous take, with Jack—having fallen asleep on a deck chair aboard a cruise ship returning from Hawaii—dreaming that Marilyn Monroe has fallen in love with him. There's great comedic chemistry as she plays off Benny's running gag about his age:

"Marilyn, I know this is sudden, but will you marry me?"

"Marry you? But look at the difference in our ages!"

"Well, there isn't much difference. You're twenty-five and I'm thirty-nine…"

"Yes, but what about twenty-five years from now when I'm fifty and you're thirty-nine?"

Marilyn played her wide-eyed Lorelei Lee image to the hilt. Before it was all over, she and Jack enjoyed a long, passionate kiss—

and the skit concluded with her performance of "Bye Bye Baby" from *Gentlemen Prefer Blondes*.

Maril's Twentieth Century-Fox contract didn't allow her to be paid for appearing on television—but it said nothing about accepting gifts. So Jack Benny gave her a black Cadillac convertible with red upholstery as his way of saying thank-you.

* * *

Maril and Joe DiMaggio seemed perfect together. Attracted to his strength and maturity, she also loved Joe's family just as she loved ours. What she initially didn't realize, however, was that he expected her to quit her career for him. In Joe's world, a woman married to become a housewife and homemaker, period. As this was a full-time job, it didn't enter his mind that Marilyn would continue making movies— while it didn't enter hers that she wouldn't.

There were other differences between them: she loved public- ity, Joe shunned the spotlight; she was uninhibited and flirtatious, he was jealous and possessive. When they dined at restaurants, fans often approached their table for an autograph—*her* autograph, not his. Though Joe was publicity-shy, it wounded his ego that Maril got all the attention.

One time, after Maril and Joe announced their engagement, she was alone at the airport, wearing an ostentatious mink coat. While photographers and fans hounded her, she went to an airline counter and phoned for help. Minutes later, one of Joe's bodyguards arrived at the airport, hustled her through the mob of fans and photographers, and drove her to Nana's house.

It was nearly dark when she knocked at our door with Joe's body- guard at her side, still frightened and shaking from her close call at the airport. I'm glad she knew our family provided a safe place where she could escape the pressures of fame. And I'm also grateful Joe had bodyguards he could dispatch whenever she needed protection. Following the airport incident, Maril often arrived at Nana's house with two bodyguards; one would stay with the car while the other accompanied her indoors.

Despite the differences between Maril and Joe, they were crazy about each other. And, when our family met Joe, we thought they made the perfect couple.

By December 1953, Maril was battling Twentieth Century-Fox over a musical comedy project called *The Girl in Pink Tights*, starring Frank Sinatra. She hated the script and, instead of reporting for work, went to San Francisco to spend Christmas with Joe and his family. Receiving word on January 4, 1954, that Fox had suspended her, Maril shrugged it off.

Nine days later, Maril called Nana to talk about her wedding plans. She was excited and so was Nana, who promised to pray for her and be there in spirit. The next day, January 14, making their way through a crowd of reporters and photographers, Marilyn and Joe climbed the steps of San Francisco's city hall. To please her new husband, Maril dressed conservatively in a dark brown suit with an ermine collar, and the ceremony itself took place in the book-lined chambers of Judge Charles S. Perry.

Joe's friends and relatives were crowded in there when he and Maril said their vows before posing for photographers. Then, after descending the city hall steps, the happy couple sped off in Joe's blue Cadillac along Highway 101 and spent their first night as husband and wife at a motel near Paso Robles.

Following their honeymoon at a mountain lodge, they returned to the DiMaggio family home in San Francisco. Joe's son from his first marriage, Joe Jr., visited from college to be with his dad and Marilyn; in addition to the three of them becoming good friends, Maril and Joe Jr. would remain close even after she and his father divorced. (Joe Jr. would be one of the last people to speak with her on the phone just hours before her death on August 4, 1962.)

In February of '54, Joe and Maril took off for a vacation in Japan. Upon their arrival, the US Army asked Maril to entertain the troops on a ten-stop tour of Korea. To Joe's dismay, she agreed. So Maril left for a few days while Joe stayed behind in Japan.

The following month, rehearsals would begin for *There's No Business Like Show Business*, a musical extravaganza built around the music of Irving Berlin. Yet, as Maril was still under suspension by Fox, she had no role in it...until Berlin dined at the home of her old benefactor, studio head Joe Schenck. As soon as the composer saw a framed photo there of Marilyn, he instinctively knew she'd be perfect for the sultry "Heat Wave" number in the movie.

Although it was after midnight, Berlin persuaded Schenck to immediately call Maril and wake her. Then he put Berlin on the phone. The songwriter's insistence on having Maril in the picture was the leverage Maril needed to end the standoff with Fox. She told the studio she'd appear in the film *if* she could also have the starring role in Billy Wilder's upcoming *The Seven Year Itch*.

Fox capitulated and lifted the suspension.

8: A WEDDING SURPRISE

THE WEDDING OF MY eighteen-year-old cousin Jacqui Warren to Herb Rigoni took place on August 8, 1954, at Saint Cyril of Jerusalem Catholic Church on Ventura Boulevard in Encino. I had just turned thirteen the previous week and was looking forward to this big family event—partly because I was excited for Jacqui, partly because Nana had told me Maril would be there.

Since Maril wanted to slip in unnoticed, Nana informed me I mustn't tell a soul. This made sense, as I'd already seen Maril getting mobbed by fans and reporters. So on the day of the wedding, while Daddy and Jane Wyman sat at the front of the church, Nana, Maril, and I snuck up the stairs to the choir loft at the back of the building. Maril wanted to be there for Jacqui, but she didn't want to be identified. She also didn't want to run into Jane and Daddy since Maril's plan was to not act as a distraction during Jacqui's big day. Truth is, I don't think Jane saw Maril come in.

This wedding really was a comedy of errors. Nana brought a family friend, Jack Petrie, upstairs to play the organ for the wedding. Jack had been drinking that day and was three sheets to the wind. He told my cousin Johnny the organ didn't work and Johnny said, "Well, you have to plug it in!" So he did and it worked!

Jack played an up-tempo, very abridged version of Wagner's "Bridal Chorus" (aka "Here Comes the Bride") while Jacqui started down the aisle with her father, Jack Warren. The father of the bride tried to keep pace with Petrie's rushed tempo, but Jacqui tugged on his arm, whispering, "Dad, this is *my* show! Slow down!"

Jacqui and her dad finally reached the altar, and Herb took his place at Jacqui's side. Father Lalor had apparently sampled the communion wine before the service, and he proceeded to mangle the wedding vows. Turning to Jacqui, he said, "Do you take this woman to be your lawfully wedded bride?" Father Lalor immediately corrected himself and said, "Do you take this *man* to be your lawfully wedded husband?"

After Father Lalor pronounced Herb and Jacqui man and wife, the guests got up and filed toward the receiving line. Nana, Maril, and I decided to sneak down the stairs and slip out of the church, hoping no one would notice Marilyn Monroe. But as Maril came down the steps, she nearly collided with Daddy and Jane.

Time stood still.

Nana gripped my arm, Maril put her hand to her mouth and gasped, Jane looked stiffly at Maril, and Daddy stared straight ahead because, in that moment, he wanted to be someplace else.

"Let's go, Fred," Jane said, coolly taking his hand.

Running to the car, they swiftly raced out of that parking lot.

Jimmy Starr, movie columnist from the *Los Angeles Herald-Express*, was our friend and his son was Johnny's buddy, who moved down the street. Sometimes Johnny had to be mindful what he said to Jimmy's son. For example, when Jacqui got married and Maril and Jane were there, that got in the paper right away. Jimmy wrote a whole article about the wedding—including the meeting at the back door between Jane Wyman and Marilyn Monroe.

Maril remained composed, promptly ignored the whole thing with Daddy and Jane, and still attended the reception at Jacqui's house. She hung out with all the guests and had several pictures taken with young men in uniform. They all wanted a photo with the famous Marilyn Monroe. She posed with them, smiled, and laughed.

"It's funny, out of all the cameramen at my wedding, not many took pictures of any kind except snapshots," says Jacqui, who didn't mind being upstaged by the movie star.

Maril's presence guaranteed no one would forget Jacqui's wedding day. Maril and Jacqui stood on either side of Herb, and Uncle Jack picked up his home movie camera and began filming. Frames from that film captured split-second moments of Maril's character that were absolutely astounding.

Marilyn Monroe in four still frames from an August 8, 1954
film shot by Jacqui Warren Rigoni's father Jack Warren at his
daughter's wedding (From the collection of Terry Karger)

When Herb wrapped one arm around his bride and the other around Maril, Jacqui was "jealously thinking, 'What's he holding *her* for? It's *my* wedding day!'"

Jacqui Warren Rigoni, Herb Rigoni, and Marilyn Monroe in a still
frame from an August 8, 1954 film shot by Jacqui's father Jack Warren
at his daughter's wedding (From the collection of Terry Karger)

At the end of the film, Maril can be seen saying, "Let's get closer," and then the camera stops. She was very careful, especially about those photos taken at the wedding. She wanted a little more involvement with the camera; Maril knew where to look and how to create a moment everyone would want to be a part of.

She understood how much Herb and Jacqui would cherish that film in the years to come. In the movie, Herb looks at one, then the other—but from the gleam in his eyes, you know his heart belongs to Jacqui.

When Maril was leaving, Johnny handed her the microphone from his tape recorder and she said, "Was this taped? I can't talk into this right now."

It had something to do with her studio contract. Everybody knew who she was, but there were no pretenses of any kind. We were simply hanging out with Maril just as we always had in the past.

"Soon after I was married, I went to a party with Maril, my mother, and Mary at Aunt Ann's apartment," Jacqui later recalled. "Marilyn and my mother, Rita Warren, sang a duet and their voices blended beautifully. At the time, having Marilyn in our lives seemed so natural, but looking back, realizing how the world was obsessed with her, calling her a 'goddess' and a 'sex symbol,' it's hard to believe she was a part of our family.

"I can still see her relaxing, lounging with one leg over the arm of the chair, laughing, and enjoying herself—no makeup, no glamour-girl poses, no cares or pressures. Around us, and especially at Auntie Ann's, she was comfortable just being herself. Ann was a very loving woman. She was like her mom."

* * *

Filming of *The Seven Year Itch* officially began on September 1, 1954, immediately after Maril finished shooting *There's No Business Like Show Business*. She went from one film to the next without even a day's break. *Itch* is the story of a beautiful girl who becomes the fantasy object of her downstairs neighbor, played by Tom Ewell. Among his fantasies: a parody of the famous kiss on the beach between Burt Lancaster and Deborah Kerr in *From Here to Eternity*. You get the idea …

Maril flew to New York on September 9 for location filming. Shooting for the most iconic moment in the picture took place between 1:00 and 3:00 a.m. on September 15. The site was a subway grate on Lexington Avenue between 52nd and 53rd Streets. As hundreds of onlookers and photographers cheered, Maril stood over the grate in a white halter dress with matching shoes and purse. Every time the subway train whooshed underneath the grate, the wind blew her pleated dress up above her hips (and sometimes above her shoulders), exposing her white panties.

Though Billy Wilder's CinemaScope cameras captured all the action, the hoots and cheers of the crowd rendered the footage unusable. Apparently, the whole shoot was nothing more than a publicity stunt. The scene was later reshot under the controlled conditions of a closed soundstage at the Twentieth Century-Fox studios in Century City—and that classic photo of Maril standing over the subway grate helped make her creation, Marilyn Monroe, an icon.

For me, it's tinged with sadness because the shoot triggered the most painful episode in Maril's marriage to Joe. Although Joe was in town that night, he hadn't planned on attending his wife's big photo session on Lexington Avenue…until his longtime friend, columnist Walter Winchell, persuaded him to go. Marilyn's dress was already billowing and the crowd cheering when Joe and Walter arrived.

Almost instantly, the Yankee Clipper became angry about what he regarded as his wife's blatantly sexual display—and the crowd's chants of "higher, higher!" definitely didn't help. Before long, he'd had enough and left without a word to his wife. Yet that night, people staying near Joe and Maril's suite at the St. Regis Hotel described hearing noises and raised voices from their room.

Maril initially refused to comment on the rumors of domestic violence or say a word against Joe. "I'm just a pretty girl who's soon forgotten," she told reporters a few days later while still in New York. "But not Joe. He's an all-time great."[32]

This forgiving attitude didn't last long; Maril and Joe loved each other, but his possessive anger convinced her she couldn't stay married to him. So within days of returning to Hollywood, she hired celebrity attorney Jerry Giesler to represent her in a divorce action.

At the time, I was thirteen, alternating between the homes of Mom in West Hollywood and Jane Wyman with Daddy in Beverly Hills. I often visited Nana. As did Maril, who'd pour her heart out while asking for Nana's advice. In fact, the only time I saw Maril angry was during the days before she divorced Joe. She used Nana's phone to call him, and I can remember how her enraged face and loud voice made me frightened for her.

Finally, she hung up—not by slamming down the phone but by just setting the receiver in its cradle while Joe was talking. He didn't call back.

The screen goddess and the baseball hero had been living in a quaint cottage at 508 North Palm Drive in Beverly Hills. On Wednesday, October 6, 1954, Joe and his friend Reno Barsocchini showed up there to clean out his possessions. As reporters lined the sidewalk, Joe loaded up the trunk and back seat of his blue Cadillac. He was angry that day—not with Maril but with himself. He knew his possessiveness had inflicted irreparable harm on the relationship, and he wished he could undo the damage. But it was too late.

Before leaving, Joe kissed Maril goodbye. Then, choking up while she was in tears, he got into his car and, with Reno behind the wheel, headed south toward Santa Monica Boulevard before vanishing from sight. Next, the front door of Maril's house opened and she stepped onto the front porch with attorney Jerry Giesler at her side, leaning on him for support.

Using a handkerchief to dab her running mascara in front of the newsreel cameras, the tragically beautiful Maril looked distraught while Giesler told reporters she and Joe were divorcing due to the demands of their conflicting careers. Three weeks later, on October 27, Maril then appeared in Santa Monica Superior Court, appropriately attired in black, accompanied by Mr. Giesler, business manager Inez Melson, columnist Sidney Skolsky, and, for moral support, Daddy's sister Mary.

At the end of the hearing, Maril was granted an uncontested divorce from Joe. Their marriage had lasted exactly 286 days.

Well aware of this crisis, Billy Wilder was kind and understanding toward Maril during the remaining weeks of filming *The Seven Year Itch*. In addition to rearranging his shooting schedule so she had time to recover, he also demonstrated patience when, after returning to work, she sometimes showed up hours late to the studio. Somehow still able to weave her magic in front of the cameras, she also appeared distracted and lost in thought between takes.

By the start of November, newspaper gossip columns were running reports about a possible reconciliation between Joe DiMaggio and Marilyn Monroe. Yet, on the fifth, Maril issued a statement through her publicist quashing the rumors.

9: AFTER YOU GET WHAT YOU WANT, YOU DON'T WANT IT

MARIL COMPLETED *THE SEVEN Year Itch* in early November 1954. The next project Fox wanted her to star in was *How to Be Very, Very Popular*—a retread of *How to Marry a Millionaire*, which had been a huge success the previous year. Both movies were written by Nunnally Johnson and costarred Betty Grable—without, in the later film's case, Marilyn Monroe.

Like any actor serious about their craft, Maril wanted to do something new. So, echoing her response when offered *The Girl in Pink Tights*, she took a walk. And, having already formulated a plan with her friend photographer Milton H. Greene to start her own company, Marilyn Monroe Productions Inc., she quickly capitalized on the breakdown of her relationship with Fox to announce its formation. Greene advised her to drop out of sight.

By this time, Aunt Mary's husband, Major Walter Short, had been transferred to Fort Monmouth, New Jersey, taking his wife and children with him. Still married to Jane Wyman, Daddy was living in Beverly Hills. And, most of the time, I was living with my mother. So Nana sold the big house on North Harper Avenue and moved to the Voltaire Apartments (now known as the Granville Towers) at 1424 North Crescent Heights in West Hollywood.

The Voltaire was home to many Hollywood celebs, including Jack Lord and Ann Sothern. So it was only natural that, disappearing from public view after divorcing Joe and ending the lease on their North

Palm Drive cottage, Maril quietly moved in with Nana. This was only a temporary arrangement, but Nana's apartment was the perfect hideout. Answering the door as well as the phone, Nana was ready to head off any reporters, private detectives, or process servers who might call—even though none actually did.

"Where is Marilyn Monroe?" screamed the newspaper headlines. "Marilyn Missing!"

Buying those papers, Nana took them back to the apartment where Maril spread them out on the floor—and they both had a big laugh. There Maril was, in the heart of Hollywood, about a twenty-minute drive from the Fox studios, and the world thought she had vanished.

Around this same time, in mid-December 1954, Fox released *There's No Business Like Show Business*. Subsequently nominated for three Academy Awards, including Best Story, it suffered harsh reviews and disappointing box office returns; today's TV viewers are far more receptive to the film than their 1950s predecessors. Yet Maril had no doubt *The Seven Year Itch* would be a hit. Leaving Hollywood to make a clean start, she relocated to the East Coast after spending a week and a half with Nana.

No longer wedded to Joe DiMaggio or Twentieth Century-Fox, Marilyn was now free to make the movies *she* wanted to make.

During her first few months on the East Coast, Maril was a houseguest of Milton and Amy Greene in Connecticut. Life with the Greenes offered many familiar experiences: a rural lifestyle, walks in the woods, picnics, and snow. Babysitting the Greenes' little boy, Joshua, Maril again enjoyed being part of a family—but this was no vacation in the woods. She was there to work.

Milton Greene spent much of 1955 negotiating with Fox to secure Maril's control of her future and her image—and he ended up hammering out an agreement that enabled Marilyn Monroe Productions Inc. to make two films: *Bus Stop* (to be distributed by Fox) and *The Prince and the Showgirl* with Laurence Olivier (to be distributed by Warner Bros.).

By March 1955, Maril had been out of the public eye for five months, ever since announcing her divorce from Joe. So she and Milton decided to reintroduce her via a Ringling Bros. and Barnum & Bailey Circus performance at Madison Square Garden, benefitting the Arthritis and Rheumatism Foundation. Also used to announce the creation of her independent movie company, this high-profile event would feature Milton Berle as ringmaster while Marilyn Monroe rode a pink elephant named Kinardy (painted pachyderm pink per her own suggestion).

After inviting our family to be there, Maril made sure we had front-row seats at the Garden on March 30, 1955—alongside Joe DiMaggio, with whom she'd decided to remain friends. When Maril appeared on the pink elephant, the crowd exploded in gasps and cheers at the sight of her dazzling ivory taffeta showgirl costume, complete with black velvet striping, trailing clouds of crepe streamers and ostrich plumes.

Thanks to the spotlights flashing brilliantly off the sequins and faux diamonds, Maril looked luminous as, seated just behind the elephant's ears, surrounded by handlers, clowns, and other performers, she laughed, waved, and blew kisses to the crowd. I didn't think she could look any happier—especially when, spotting us with Joe, her eyes widened with joy.

There were many other amazing acts that night, but for me they're just a blur. How could anyone compete with Maril's entrance atop an elephant in shades of pink, ivory, and platinum blonde?

.

10: THE DEVILISH TRIO

THE SEVEN YEAR ITCH premiered June 1, 1955, at Loew's State Theatre on Times Square. To promote this event, the studio transformed the subway grate photo of Maril with her billowing dress into a fifty-foot-high billboard above the Loew's marquee—and she confessed to us that she drove past the theater several times to stare in amazement at the oversized image of herself.

Soon after the premiere, Maril returned to California to continue publicizing the film, which, being an instant hit with critics and audiences, gave her the upper hand in her negotiations with Twentieth Century-Fox. Meanwhile, Maril also took this opportunity to reconnect with Aunt Mary and my mother Patti—the three referred to as the Devilish Trio because Maril the prankster often involved Mom and Mary in her escapades. Maril's nickname for Aunt Mary was Buddynuts.

One night in June 1955, the Devilish Trio were out well past midnight, talking about old times, when Maril suggested driving to Grauman's Chinese Theatre. So they headed over to Hollywood Boulevard and, after pulling up to the curb, Mom stayed with the car as a lookout while Maril and Aunt Mary ran to the forecourt—passing the concrete paving on which Maril and Jane Russell had etched their signatures two years earlier. Near the main entrance, they snatched the life-size *Seven Year Itch* cutout of Marilyn in her white dress, hurried with it back to the car, and sped the twenty minutes toward Jane Wyman's home at 333 South Beverly Glen Boulevard, where they placed that cutout in the middle of the front lawn before disappearing into the night.

Jane and Daddy had separated on November 7, 1954, an interlocutory divorce decree had been granted a month later on December 7, and it would become final on the thirtieth of December in 1955.

Jane Wyman appeared in Santa Monica Superior Court on December 7, 1954, where she was granted an interlocutory divorce decree from Fred Karger (Associated Press)

Jane Wyman at Santa Monica Superior Court on December 7, 1954 (United Press)

So the prank targeted my stepmother Jane—not Daddy—and while she wasn't amused, Maril was tickled pink.

Here's a bit of irony: Though my mother Patti helped Maril pull off the cutout prank on Jane Wyman's front lawn, Jane and Mom were friends. As fellow ex-wives of Freddie Karger, they had a lot in common.

I remember that in early 1981, around the time of Ronald Reagan's inauguration, Jane called my mother and told her she had been cast in the lead role in *Falcon Crest* (1981–1990), a new nighttime soap opera (in the *Dallas* and *Dynasty* genre). Mom was thrilled for her. The show was a hit, and Jane's career experienced a decade-long resurgence.

Jane Wyman on the TV show *Falcon Crest* (1981–1990) while her ex-husband Ronald Reagan was president of the United States for two terms

My mother was a smoker, and in the early 1990s she was diagnosed with lung cancer. A couple days before Mom died, Jane Wyman called her and they talked about old times and said a final goodbye. Mom passed away on May 27, 1993, in Orange County, California.

I'm sure Jane knew at the time that Mom had helped Maril pull off the prank on Jane's front lawn. Knowing Mom, she confessed her part in the stunt, and she and Jane had a good laugh over it. Again, as Louella Parsons said, Jane was a "good scout."

* * *

Maril's mischievous side has rarely been reported in Marilyn Monroe biographies and documentaries. Yet my family witnessed it many times, including when, driving Mom and Aunt Mary in her black Cadillac convertible, Maril was spotted by Frank Sinatra steering his own convertible in the opposite direction. Beside him was actor Peter Lawford, and both men waved and shouted at her as they drove past.

"Bye, guys!" she called back, flooring the accelerator. This prompted Sinatra to hang a U-turn and give chase, but he was no match for Maril racing along the boulevard.

"Are they still behind us?" she asked after a few minutes.

"You've lost them," Mom replied. "Who taught you to drive like that?"

"I've had plenty of practice being chased by photographers," Maril explained, slowing down.

One Halloween, I was with Ben and Anne. Maril was there, too, along with Mother and Mary. Instead of asking for candy, Mary chimed in and said, "Hey, how about we ask for Scotch and champagne?!"

Then there was the time when, dating Packard Bell Electronics exec Howard Thomas following her divorce from Daddy, Mom couldn't think of a gift for Howard's birthday. Living in a big house with a pool in West LA, he was very well off. So Mom faced the old dilemma—what to get the man who has everything?—until she hit upon a bright idea.

Arriving at Howard's place with Aunt Mary and an oversize package, my mother rang the front doorbell and both women shouted, "Happy birthday!" as soon as he appeared.

"Don't just stand there," Mom exclaimed. "Open your present!"

Positioned between her and Aunt Mary, the present was loosely wound in layers of shiny cellophane. So Howard unwrapped it...and was greeted by Marilyn Monroe wearing a white dress with a big red ribbon tied in a huge bow.

"Thanks, Howard," she said wide-eyed in her breathiest Marilyn voice. "It was getting kinda stuffy in there. Happy birthday!"

Maril planted a big kiss on his startled face, and that sealed the deal. It was a birthday Howard would never forget.

11: JOE WAS FAMILY

JOE DiMAGGIO GREW CLOSER to the Kargers during the months following his divorce from Maril. One evening in 1955, he visited Nana at the Voltaire Apartments and opened his heart to her about how devastated he felt over the breakup—in front of her brother John and my awkward-feeling father.

It wasn't easy for Daddy to hear Joe say he still loved Maril while admitting his possessiveness and rage on the night of the subway-grate incident had destroyed their marriage. Nothing her ex-lover could say to her ex-husband would help him feel better. So, leaving Joe to talk with Nana and Uncle John, Daddy stepped away from the conversation, sat down at the piano, and played softly in the background.

Here was the great Joe DiMaggio, one of America's most admired men, wallowing in regret and self-reproach in Nana's living room. Well aware Daddy was Maril's first love and that she never quite got over him, the recent Baseball Hall of Fame inductee consumed enough drinks that night to magnify his own pain. And after Aunt Mary's family moved to Fort Monmouth, New Jersey, he continued to stay in touch.

Frequently in the New York–New Jersey area due to his association with the Yankees, Joe would call or visit whenever he was nearby. Aunt Mary and the Kargers were a link to Maril, and he didn't want that link to be broken.

Frank Dalton, the son of Aunt Mary's milkman, recalled the time he met Maril at Mary's house in New Jersey. "My father was a milkman for Farmers and Consumers Dairy in Morristown, New Jersey," Frank said. "In 1955, after I had just turned sixteen, he was telling everybody how he had Marilyn Monroe on his route. I begged him to take me along on his milk route, which started at four o'clock in the morning.

"Sure enough, we went to [Mary Karger's] house in New Jersey. My father knocked on the door, dropping off two quarts of homogenized milk, and Marilyn Monroe answered it at the side or back door to the house.

"My dad said, 'I'd like you to meet my son Frankie.' She said, 'Nice to meet you,' and she put out her hand and gave a little nod of the head. She had a cigarette in the other hand and she had a bathrobe on. Her hair was in a few curlers. She didn't have much makeup on but she sure was pretty, I can tell you that!"

"In 1955, when my father was stationed at Fort Monmouth, Andy Griffith was starring in *No Time for Sergeants* on Broadway," my cousin Ben recalls. "Joe DiMaggio brought all four of us to New York, put us up in a hotel for the night, and treated us to dinner and a Broadway show. It was a military comedy, and Joe knew my stepfather, Walter, would really enjoy it. Our family felt especially close to Joe after that. In fact, Joe DiMaggio and my mother Mary became golfing buddies, and Joe used to come down whenever he was on the East Coast to golf with Mom at Fort Monmouth.

"In 1996, I went back to Little Silver, New Jersey, for my fortieth high school reunion. I visited that small house again, and the new owners already knew about Marilyn. Apparently it came with the real estate. They said, 'Marilyn Monroe was in this house and so was Joe DiMaggio.'"

12: A METHOD TO THE MADNESS

MARIL DIDN'T MAKE ANY movies in 1955. Instead, having left drama coach Natasha Lytess behind in Hollywood, she spent most of the year refining her craft under the tutelage of Lee and Paula Strasberg at the Actors Studio—studying the "Method" style of acting originally conceived by Konstantin Stanislavski, summoning real emotions from within.

When Major Walter Short and Aunt Mary moved to New Jersey, Maril began visiting from New York. She knew Ben wanted to become an actor and, because he was old enough to study at the Actors Studio, Maril told his parents she'd sponsor him there and let him stay at her Manhattan apartment. Unfortunately, Walter declined the offer and Ben didn't hear a word about it…until years later when he was understandably very upset.

The Actors Studio transformed Maril's approach to her craft. The exercises she underwent and insights she gained greatly increased her depth and range as an actress. Up to that time, acting for her had more or less been a game of "let's pretend," learning a set of skills, tricks, and techniques. The Actors Studio taught her to dive deep into her troubled psyche and emotional pain. Instead of make-believe, acting became about truth—her *hidden* truth.

As such, although learning the Method was an enormous help to Marilyn the actress, I don't think it benefited Maril the human being. One of the disciplines Lee Strasberg put her through was the so-called sense memory exercise that, when recalling a past incident, required her to describe everything she was sensing: sights, sounds, smells, even dialogue; no feelings, only the memory-related sensory input. The mere act of expressing those sensations would summon the emotions.

Some of Maril's classmates said that she did exactly as Strasberg directed; without her description of a particular event, none of them knew what she was recalling—but they *did* soon witness her uncontrollable sobbing. Instead of offering emotional support, the drama coach just provided a clinical evaluation of her performance. It may well have felt like he was trampling on her childhood pain with muddy shoes—which is why reconnecting with excruciating memories to convey authentic feelings probably caused psychological damage.

Subsequently urging Maril to undergo Freudian psychoanalysis, the Strasbergs recommended Hungarian analyst Dr. Marianne Kris—while Milton Greene referred her to Dr. Margaret Hohenberg. However, the cost of those sessions was so high, Maril had to move from the Waldorf Towers to a less expensive apartment.

The Strasbergs and the psychiatrists were playing with forces in Maril's life that they didn't understand. By exposing her fragile, wounded soul—ripping open the wounds of her orphanage years and childhood sexual abuse—they unleashed emotional toxins she couldn't endure without the anesthetic of drink and drugs. And in so doing, they helped transform this beautiful creature from a good actress to a great actress—an actress who flashed across the heavens like a meteor; brilliant for a moment, gone all too soon.

Many movie industry skeptics ridiculed Maril for studying at the Actors Studio, berating her as a "dumb blonde" who foolishly thought she could act. Those skeptics made a common mistake: they confused Maril with the roles she played. They saw her play Lorelei Lee in *Gentlemen Prefer Blondes* or Pola Debevoise in *How to Marry a Millionaire* and assumed Marilyn Monroe was just as ditzy in real life. Maril, however, was smarter than most of her critics. As she once said, "I don't mind if people *think* I'm a dumb blonde, but I dread the thought of *being* a dumb blonde."[33]

Maril achieved what she did precisely because she knew what she was doing. She had good instincts and well-planned goals, and she was focused on getting what she wanted—including the chance to prove herself as an actress. Yet this bright, articulate woman had to put up with the stupidity of studio bosses who kept offering her the same stereotyped roles, movie after movie—then tried to punish her when she resisted.

Studio execs may have underestimated her when negotiating, film critics often underestimated her in their reviews, but moviegoers soon discovered Marilyn Monroe was an actress of great range, intelligence, and emotional depth. A case in point: *Bus Stop*. She had already demonstrated a talent for the dramatic in *Clash by Night* and *Don't Bother to Knock* (as a convincingly disturbed babysitter), and she was improving all the time.

"Look, I'm a woman," Maril told Leo Guild in a 1959 interview, mirroring much of what she had told Pete Martin three years earlier. "Sex is a part of nature and I'm part of nature. I don't understand all the whispers about the subject. I don't do anything that's wrong—I just behave as a female. What's wrong with that? ...I want better parts, better directors, better writers and I don't care about money ...I want to be an actress. I want to be an artist. I am qualified and I want to prove it."[34]

Which she did.

* * *

"Of all the stars you've worked with, who's the most elegant?" I once asked my suave, sophisticated father. Without hesitation, he said, "Tyrone Power."

In August and September 1955, Daddy worked with Power on a biopic called *The Eddy Duchin Story*. The title character, portrayed by Power, was a 1930s and '40s bandleader who died at age forty-two from leukemia. Because Duchin was known for his virtuosity as a pianist, Daddy gave Power lessons in that department. And he also worked with composer George Duning on the film's musical score.

During filming, I flew to New York, visited Daddy on the set, and was introduced to Victoria Shaw, who had a key supporting role in the picture. Some scenes were filmed in Central Park and others at the Waldorf Astoria where, as Daddy knew, Maril was then living. So, recalling her saying she'd like to meet Tyrone Power, he phoned her and offered to introduce them at a party for the cast and crew.

She sounded excited to meet one of her favorite stars. As arranged, Daddy showed up at Maril's ground-floor apartment at eight o'clock that night to escort her to the party, but when he phoned her from the front desk, she said she wasn't ready. A couple of hours passed before Maril called Daddy; instead of sounding excited as she had earlier, she sounded hazy and scattered. Daddy realized she'd been drinking—and, aware she was in no shape to meet people, told her to get some rest.

Some who were close to Maril during her New York years believe she started seriously abusing prescription barbiturates and combining them with alcohol around 1955, when she began studying at the Actors Studio. It doesn't take a giant leap of the imagination to surmise she used them to drown her insecurities and anesthetize painful memories that were daily being revived in her acting exercises.

Though Daddy was frustrated about Maril not accompanying him to the party, he didn't understand her emotional turmoil or know about the powerful meds she was taking to deaden her pain.

13: BUS STOP

MARILYN MONROE'S COMEBACK MOVIE began filming on March 3, 1956. Armed with a new Fox contract that, among other things, enabled her to select the actors, writers, and directors with whom she'd work, Maril chose highly regarded Broadway and Hollywood luminary Joshua Logan to direct her as Chérie in *Bus Stop*. It was a challenging role, requiring the glamorous Maril to convincingly portray a disheveled blonde singer whose dreams are bigger than her talent. And she pulled it off brilliantly, conveying fragile desperation while maintaining her inner radiance.

Marilyn Monroe on Don Murray's shoulders by William
Woodfield on the set of *Bus Stop* in 1956

When Chérie delivers her rendition of "That Old Black Magic"—recorded live on the soundstage, not lip-synched—she is appealing and sympathetic. We like her, care for her, and hurt for her. Convinced Maril deserved the Best Actress Oscar, Josh Logan likened her to Greta Garbo.

Don Murray, meanwhile, made his motion picture debut as Beauregard "Beau" Decker, an innocent cowboy determined to win Chérie's heart. A conscientious objector during the Korean War, Murray spent nearly three years doing alternative service in post–World War II Europe, helping orphans and other victims of the conflict.

"I was out of the country and missed the whole Marilyn phenomenon," he'd recall. "In the early fifties, big stars to me were Sophia Loren in Italy when Marilyn was becoming famous. I had done live television. As her reputation goes, Marilyn was always late and that gave everybody less time to work on the scenes. She would also lose her concentration. Logan had to do scenes in little bits and pieces, so it was difficult to keep the emotion in the scene and to keep a consistent character."

Maril's lateness, we now know, was caused by the intense, chronic stage fright she battled throughout her career—and which manifested itself physically.

"As soon as Marilyn stepped out before the camera, she broke out in a strawberry rash and they covered it with makeup," Murray continued. "It didn't really show so much on her face. It was on her body. They wanted to portray a girl who was a honky-tonk singer, so she worked at night and slept during the day. Marilyn never saw the sun. That's why they wanted her pale and white in contrast to myself, who was the outdoor cowboy."

Bus Stop was Maril's first film since breaking away from Natasha Lytess.

"Marilyn's new coach, Paula Strasberg, was helpful," Murray said. "Joshua Logan worked with her. Instead of resenting her, he used her for added help with Marilyn. But he didn't have Paula working on the set. She was always off the set when working with Marilyn, then she'd come on and Josh Logan would take over from there and direct her. Paula didn't interfere with what Logan was doing and she was helpful in preparing Marilyn for each scene.

"Logan always instructed the cinematographer: 'Nobody says "cut" around here but me, no matter what happens. We're rolling until I say "cut," because we have to put her performance together from many pieces. You never know what piece might work, and that's for me to decide, nobody else.' So he didn't cut the whole time."

One of the lessons Maril learned at the Actors Studio was the importance of remaining in character both on and off the set.

"All the times Marilyn was on the set, she would talk like that with the Ozark accent," Murray remembered. "And she would keep up her emotional intensity. In the scene where her character tells my character off, and she's about to run away, I reached for her and grabbed hold of her costume, which caused it to rip off. She turned to me and said, 'You ain't got the brains they give a monkey! Now give me back my tail!'

"All of a sudden in the take, which she didn't do in rehearsal, she ran up to me and started pounding on my chest. The first time, I wasn't prepared for it, and she knocked me out of the camera and lighting range. We had to cut and start over.

"Josh Logan said to me, 'Don, listen, she's very emotional. I don't want to disturb that. No matter what she does, just stand your ground. Put one foot behind the other.' The next take, I put one foot behind the other and when Marilyn hit my chest, she bounced off. I bent down and picked her up. I got totally out of character and I said, 'Are you all right, Marilyn?' She got up looking dazed, then she went on with the scene. After that, she ran off.

"A little later, she returned to the set and said, 'Was that all right?' I said, 'Wait a minute, that might have been good for Marilyn but it was no good for me!' I lost my character and my accent. I thought she might have hurt herself. She said, 'Oh, gosh, can't you ab-lib?' Not ad-lib but *ab*-lib. The next time we did the scene, she was still angry so she lashed me across the face with the sequins from her dress and cut my eyelid. Then she ran off."

Murray was understandably angry Maril had struck him so hard. However, she remained in character the entire time. So, when Logan asked her to apologize, she ignored the director's appeals. If Chérie wouldn't apologize, why should *she*? Don Murray wasn't amused, but he fully recognized her special radiance in front of the camera:

"The cast—Hope Lange, Betty Field, Art O'Connell, and I—all came from Broadway, so we were used to sustaining a performance instead of doing it in little bits and pieces. Marilyn never seemed to be able to make two sentences meet without losing her concentration. We all thought her performance was going to be a disaster. Instead, with the magic of movies, editor Bill Reynolds did an incredible job of editing all those little pieces of Marilyn's performance.

"We were stunned when we saw the completed film. Her performance turned out splendid. We thought, 'How wonderful she was in it.' As a matter of fact, I was nominated for an Academy Award for it and she was sadly never nominated. When they told me I was nominated, a publicist came in and said, 'Congratulations!' I said, 'For what?' 'Don't you know? You were nominated for the Academy Award... Isn't that amazing?' I said, 'Why, because I was so terrible?' 'No,' he replied, 'because nobody was pushing for you.'

"That was the most unusual thing about it. Nobody had taken out any ads or anything. It was just a spontaneous nomination. That almost never happens. I thought Marilyn not only deserved a nomination, I thought she deserved the Academy Award because her performance had much more variety and much more interest than Ingrid Bergman's *Anastasia* [which won Best Actress that year].

"Marilyn was a wonderful musical comedy performer. She moved very well and her singing voice was like a purring kitten. 'That Old Black Magic' is one of the great cinematic treasures. That thing could be preserved by itself. Her character, Chérie, is so wonderfully inept at performing and so grateful for a cowboy who shuts everybody up. It was an absolute gem.

"I was surprised Marilyn had to go to the Actors Studio to learn how to act because I had seen her in *All About Eve*. In that film, I thought she was a very good actress playing a bad actress. I thought, 'What do you mean she's got to learn how to act? Why?'

"Off the set, we didn't talk about acting. Marilyn would bring up things in her personal life without telling me what they were. She was doing things at thirty that most of us go through in our late teens. Marilyn would talk to me about Freud. She said to me, 'Do you think a leopard can change its spots?' Marilyn was obviously referring to her man and her impending marriage to Arthur Miller, although she didn't say that. It wasn't commonly known at the time, but she was having an affair with Arthur Miller."

14: MARIL SMOKED A CIGARETTE (NOT MARIJUANA) IN OUR FAMILY FILM

THIS CHAPTER MAY NOT seem important, but since misinformation is floating around the internet, my family and I feel it is our duty to clear up any falsities. One involves our 1956 family film, which many have said showed Marilyn Monroe smoking marijuana. That is vastly untrue. It was only a cigarette, nothing else.

Marilyn Monroe in 1956 at Mary Short's New Jersey house
from two still frames of a film shot by Ben's stepfather
Walter Short (From the collection of Terry Karger)

"I don't hurt anyone intentionally," Maril once said. "Why should anyone want to hurt me or my career? ...I think some of the things they write tell me more about them than they tell other people about me."[35]

Years ago, my late cousin Anne had a childhood friend by the name of Gretchen. Gretchen claims to have met Marilyn more times than she actually did.

"Marilyn was a sweetheart," Gretchen said. "She was a friend of mine. She was so different in person. She was a great gal. When she hung around with us, she was in sweats and no makeup. She was just an everyday person."

Gretchen falsely claimed responsibility for shooting our family film, which many asserted showed Maril, my cousin Anne, and my Aunt Mary smoking pot. Gretchen chuckled when asked if it was marijuana, implying this falsehood bore a resemblance to the truth.

"I'm not going to say for sure," Gretchen gleefully giggled. "Take a look at the tape and decide for yourself."

In reality, Gretchen only had a VHS copy of the film, which has since been edited. The altered film did not show the full frame, so conclusions could be drawn from this, which were untrue. She did not shoot the film as she claims, and the original was *not* on VHS and it was not an 8 mm film. It was a 16 mm film that was taken by my uncle, Walter Short.

Gretchen was obviously nowhere in the actual film! Without our family's permission, Gretchen sold the inauthentic copy of the original for an astoundingly hefty sum of $275,000!

"That's our house in New Jersey," Ben remembered. "My stepfather Walter Short took that film, *not* Gretchen. My mother Mary was very anti-marijuana. She never tried it. If you look carefully, Marilyn wasn't inhaling. My sister Anne was sixteen at the time, and her best friend was not Gretchen. It was Carolyn Bell.

"Carolyn's father was a general. My mother was married to a captain in the US Army, and Walter Short would have been out on his butt if the army thought his wife was smoking marijuana. Later, when she was married to Lowell Race, he was too straitlaced to even think about smoking dope, let alone having his wife smoke it. I was in the room and actually in the complete film. I know for a fact it was not marijuana because I was there! And another person shown in the full film was my father's boss, Colonel Charles Robertson. If he saw any member of my family smoking marijuana, my dad would have been in Fort Leavenworth prison, the infamous army prison.

"If you look at what's on YouTube, the handsome woman sitting next to Marilyn on the couch is my mother Mary, and the little girl is my sister Anne. Anne wasn't a woman at that time. She was only sixteen.

"I love this thing about Gretchen being in New Jersey. That's so patently a lie because that was 1956, and the only people in that room with Marilyn are my stepfather Captain Walter Short (who shot the film), my mother Mary, my sister Anne, my best friend Alan Peterson (in the room but not captured on camera), my girlfriend Dee Maddox, Colonel Charles 'Chuck' Robertson, and his wife Elizabeth 'Betty' Robertson. Gretchen never visited us in New Jersey.

Friend of the Family in 1956 with Betty Robertson, Marilyn Monroe, and Mary Short in Mary's New Jersey house (From the collection of Terry Karger)

Marilyn Monroe with Ben's sister Anne in 1956 at Mary Short's
New Jersey house (From the collection of Terry Karger)

Marilyn Monroe in 1956 at Mary Short's New Jersey
house (From the collection of Terry Karger)

Marilyn Monroe does shy (From the collection of Terry Karger)

"Indeed, I have the original 16 mm film, much of which was not broadcast on YouTube. Gretchen was just trying to get some money. I never gave anybody permission to sell it, use it, look at it, or anything. I have the complete film in my possession. I made two VHS copies of that film. I gave a VHS copy to my sister Anne and one to her daughter Elyse.

"My niece Elyse, who was the executer of Anne's will, was looking for Anne's copy after my sister died [on November 23, 1997] so she could have it for the family. It was gone, and she just assumed I had taken it…I do know that Gretchen did visit Anne in Palm Springs a few days before she died. Gretchen went through the house and stole the damn thing. Anne was terribly sick with lung cancer, and in that condition, she would never have given the video to Gretchen. The bad copy version shown on the internet has been edited. Stuff has been cut out. My dad's boss Chuck and his wife Betty were there along with me and my girlfriend Dee (all of which got cut out) and my best friend Alan (present but not filmed).

"I have a still photo of Marilyn with another officer named Colonel Jaeger [on the same day that film was shot with the cigarette in her hand], who was also stationed in Fort Monmouth, New Jersey.

Marilyn Monroe with Colonel Jaeger at Mary Short's house in New Jersey (Ben is in the background picture) (From the collection of Terry Karger)

"You wouldn't dare smoke marijuana back in those days in the army and not expect to go to prison. This marijuana crap is disgracing my mother, my sister, and poor Marilyn. If they were smoking marijuana in the house, everybody would have known it.

"The original film is much longer and looks fabulous, nothing like the one on the internet. It's a color Kodachrome, which is just really wonderful... There was a colonel [Charles 'Chuck' Robertson] along with his wife [Elizabeth 'Betty' Robertson] in the room! It shows him lighting up a cigarette. He's not in uniform, but he certainly is there.

"Another false allegation was that the FBI borrowed Gretchen's copy in the sixties to study it. That's ludicrous because the VHS copies didn't exist then, and nobody's possessed the original of our film of Marilyn with our family but my stepfather Walter Short and me!"

Ben's wife Jill said, "Gretchen was fifteen back then, and marijuana was not easy to get in the fifties. She lives in Oregon now, not in New Jersey. I don't know what she 'retrieved' from her 'storage spot,' but Ben has the original film, including the package it was mailed in from his stepfather Walter, who shot it. A really bad copy was stolen because in the original, the pictures are clear and sharp as a bell."

My cousin Johnny pointed out, "You have to be absolutely sure you have the original when you're working with this stuff. I used to work at the Mission San Miguel Museum as a curator. I deal with archives and manuscripts. To an archivist, it's a mortal sin. It's terrible! It was a fun family film. It wasn't anything else. Gretchen was never in New Jersey. Anne sent a letter to my mom Rita and said she had a brain tumor and was not expected to live for more than a few months. That's what I was told. I remember my mom calling me about it."

Ben recalled, "Anne's lung cancer had metastasized to her brain. Towards the end, she was going to go in for lung surgery, telling her they could take one lung out and she'd be okay. Except the night before that, a different doctor came in and looked at her, and said, 'You can't have an operation. Both of your lungs are completely involved with cancer.'"

Johnny added, "I was shocked, and during that period, that's when Gretchen got ahold of the video version of that piece of film. Ben has the original. They were smoking a cigarette…Marilyn would never do marijuana. Walter Short had a movie camera and he shot that film, not Gretchen. It was a Bell and Howell and it took one-hundred-foot reels of 16 mm film. He used to make home movies all the time when I was a kid. He had reels and reels of home movies that he had shot."

Anne's son Darrill asserted, "My mom never tried marijuana in her life. Gretchen sold that for $275,000?!"

* * *

Gretchen made more absurd allegations, falsely interjecting herself into Marilyn's last few days alive. As for August 2, 1962, Gretchen claimed, "Marilyn told me she thought somebody was going to kill her. I'm sure she knew who it was, but she didn't tell us. My girlfriend Anne and I spent the night with her because Marilyn was afraid to be by herself. We were both teenagers and Marilyn was a real good friend of Anne and her family, and she just asked if we could spend the night with her."

Johnny countered, "That's a whole made-up story."

Ben agreed. "Marilyn would never have called Gretchen two days before she died. Gretchen and my sister slept over at Marilyn's? That's baloney!"

Gretchen also seemed uncertain of the date she and Anne supposedly spent the night at Marilyn's. She wasn't sure if the date was August 2 or 3, 1962. Gretchen said, "It was so many years ago. Don't even ask me the dates. I was a teenager."

Ben shot back, "So Gretchen said they were teenagers visiting Marilyn? In 1962, my sister was twenty-two and I'm sure Gretchen was close to the same age, so they weren't teenagers. [Gretchen was twenty-one at the time.] Gretchen's story is fabricated. Every bit of it. In fact, Anne, her husband Cherrill Consoli, my nephew Darrill, and I shared a house. Anne in '62 was dancing up in Reno at Harrah's!"

My family friend Toni Dwiggins added additional support by stating, "Anne ended up being an extra in movies and a showgirl in Las Vegas. Anne was like a big sister to me that I idolized, and we also knew each other as adults. She was one of the sweetest people I have ever known. She was loving and had a huge heart, was fun, and had an infectious laugh. She was a heavy smoker, but I grew up in a haze of smoke because everybody smoked.

"My dad was a pilot and one time flew us to Reno where she was a showgirl. She was a very, very pretty woman and well suited for that. My dad, Donald Dwiggins, was a writer as well and was interviewing another pilot up there. He took me along so I could see Anne. I was fourteen or fifteen. I couldn't go to the shows because I was too young. My dad and I went to an early morning breakfast after Anne and her fellow showgirls finished their work. Of course they watched what they said around me because I was a young girl."

* * *

Gretchen was asked whether she told anyone that she or Anne saw Bobby Kennedy and Marilyn smoking marijuana together at Marilyn's house, and she readily denied the claims.

Gretchen replied, "No, no. I don't even know what you're talking about."

Maril herself said, "There is very little one can do about printed untruths… But I learned long ago that you have to take the bad with the good. And that it doesn't pay to lose your temper when untruths are printed. Sooner or later, the truth always comes out."[36]

15: THE PRINCE AND THE SHOWGIRL

MARIL POSSESSED A STRONG set of moral principles she refused to compromise. Intensely loyal to her friends, she wasn't greedy or materialistic in the slightest. Money, to her, was just something she used to make other people happy. Yes, she had known luxury and appreciated the finer things in life, but she was also perfectly content to live simply and frugally.

Maril had great compassion for children, animals, and people who were treated unjustly. As a child, like others my age, I loved her very much—so much that I wanted her to be my stepmother. Meanwhile, unable to ever turn away from a child in need, she always did whatever she could to help. And she displayed similar empathy toward adults.

As a starlet, Maril could have married her agent Johnny Hyde when he begged her to; by the end of 1950 she would have been a very rich widow. No way, however, would she exploit Johnny's love for her. Doing so would have completely contradicted her moral principles. Such a strong moral stance deserves our respect.

* * *

Ever since their first encounter in 1951, Arthur Miller and Maril had been carrying on a long-distance relationship through letters, phone calls, and occasional trysts. But it was only after Maril moved to the East Coast in 1955 that their relationship turned into an intensely passionate affair. In early 1956, when not attending classes at the

Actors Studio, she often dined with Miller or cycled alongside him in Central Park—pursuing the celebrated playwright not only for his intellect but also to fulfill her own emotional needs. I feel so sorry she was never able to meet that need.

During this time, Arthur Miller told his wife Mary—his high school sweetheart and the mother of his children—that he was ending their marriage so he could be with Maril. The divorce became final on June 11 of that year. Eighteen days later, Arthur and Marilyn married in a civil ceremony; a Jewish ceremony followed two days later, conducted in the home of Miller's literary agent Kay Brown.

The narrative in the media was that a brilliant intellectual had married a beautiful-but-dumb actress (*Variety* headlined its coverage of the wedding, "Egghead Weds Hourglass"). This makes me very upset, but this was not the Maril we knew for fourteen years. Ignorant people are incapable of distinguishing a thoughtful, intelligent actress from her film roles. This is what she feared: to be *perceived* as a dumb blonde when in fact she wasn't.

On July 13, 1956, the newlyweds departed for London, accompanied by Maril's acting coach Paula Strasberg. The trip to England was both a honeymoon and a business trip, as Maril was scheduled to begin filming *The Prince and the Showgirl* at Pinewood Studios on August 7. Her costar and director would be Laurence Olivier, who, with his wife Vivien Leigh, greeted the Millers at London Airport alongside a throng of reporters and photographers.

The film was based on Terence Rattigan's play *The Sleeping Prince*, which Olivier had performed opposite Leigh on the London stage, portraying a prince regent attempting to convince a showgirl to fall in love with him. Initially enchanted with the prospect of playing opposite Marilyn Monroe, the acclaimed thespian soon ran into one of the most maddening experiences of his career. As a Shakespearean actor, Olivier didn't approve of the Actors Studio's Method approach, resented Paula Strasberg's constant on-set presence, and was driven to distraction by Maril's chronic lateness and frequent inability to follow his directions.

Despite these frustrations, Olivier completed production on schedule and under budget. What's more, even though he found it sheer agony to work with Maril, he later praised her performance before the cameras.

During a break in production for *The Prince and the Showgirl*, Maril returned to the United States, spending time with Arthur Miller in both New York and Hollywood. Jill D'Aubery, my cousin Ben's wife and the daughter of actor Roland Varno, encountered Maril by pure chance in October 1956 during the actress's California visit.

"I was almost sixteen and a fan of Marilyn's, as most teenage girls were," she recalls. "I practically wanted to *be* her. Then, one day, strolling down Hollywood Boulevard, I saw this woman walking toward me, wearing Levi's, a man's shirt tied in front, sandals, and a headscarf. As she passed by, something about her struck me as breathtaking. So I turned around and followed her into a little store, where she looked at a costume jewelry counter. Then she removed her headscarf, turned around, saw me standing by the doorway, and smiled. It was Marilyn!

"I stood there with my mouth open, staring at probably the most beautiful creature I'd ever seen in my entire life. Not a bit of makeup, hair kind of tousled—she was gorgeous and very gentle, like a fawn. That's the one and only time I ever saw her."

During this same trip to Hollywood, Maril stopped by the Voltaire Apartments to visit Nana and me—and tell us she'd been invited to a Royal Command Performance of the motion picture *The Battle of the River Plate* at the Empire cinema on Central London's Leicester Square. Maril was nervous about her upcoming October 29 introduction there to Queen Elizabeth II—even though the monarch was just over a month older than the screen icon. How should she act? What should she say? And how could she calm the butterflies inside her?

Nana's advice was simple: "Look the queen straight in the eye and say to yourself, 'I'm just as pretty as you are.'"[37]

I remember Maril listening to Nana's words of wisdom before practicing her curtsey until she felt she had it down. The following day she flew back to England and, butterflies notwithstanding, conducted herself with poise and grace in the presence of royalty.

* * *

Production of both *Bus Stop* and *The Prince and the Showgirl* had been plagued by Maril's well-known habit of arriving late to the set and forgetting her lines. Was her worsening memory a symptom of her increasing barbiturate use? Third husband Arthur Miller thought so. And it breaks my heart that so many of her understandably aggravated directors and costars were critical of behaviors that spoke to Maril's deeper problems—including the emotional pain constantly exposed by the Actors Studio and psychoanalysis, as well as the pills and alcohol she took as an anesthetic. It seemed everyone around her was either furious with her or taking advantage of her. Who was trying to help?

Bus Stop was filmed from March through May 1956, *The Prince and the Showgirl* from August to mid-November. Maril then took a year and a half off from work while she and Arthur divided their time between three residences: an apartment in Manhattan, an eighteenth-century farmhouse in Connecticut, and a summer home in Amagansett on Long Island. The children from his first marriage were twelve-year-old Jane and nine-year-old Robert, who, after college, would work as a production assistant on numerous Hollywood films while also directing commercials.

When, in 1990, the film rights would become available to his father's play *The Crucible*, Robert would option the property and produce the movie for Twentieth Century-Fox six years later. Arthur would receive an Oscar nomination for writing the script—having penned the original stage play after beginning his affair with Maril in 1951. As Robert studied that play, he was amazed to discover much of its power derived from the emotional realism of the author's guilt-wracked protagonist, John Proctor, having an affair with a young seductress in old Salem. This, Robert realized, was Arthur himself, agonizing over his relationship with Maril and the betrayal of his own marriage.

Robert Miller said, "I was very moved by the scenes about betrayal and forgiveness in a marriage."[38] He has made few public statements about the nearly five years he spent as Marilyn Monroe's stepson. "I was quite young at the time, and I remember we used to play some badminton. There are other memories, but I'd just as soon keep those personal. I can certainly appreciate and understand the attention she continues to draw. I think she'd probably be astonished by it all, but also very pleased to see a lot of it, and not so pleased to see some of it. I enjoyed being with her, and she was a lovely friend to me."

In June 1957, while in Amagansett, Maril learned she was pregnant. It was a dream come true, and she excitedly called Nana with the news, remarking, "I've never been happier than I am right now."

Six weeks later, her joy turned to despair. While puttering in her garden on August 1, Maril suffered an attack of abdominal pain. Finding her doubled up on the ground, writhing and screaming, Arthur rushed her to the doctor, who determined she had an ectopic pregnancy—the embryo had attached to the fallopian tube instead of the interior of the uterus, meaning the pregnancy had to be terminated to save her life.

Maril had invested her hopes for happiness in becoming a mother. For a few short weeks, it had looked like her dream was finally coming true, yet it ended in pain, surgery, and sadness.

One night in early September 1957, Miller noticed Maril sleeping on a chair, struggling to breathe, and recognized the symptoms of her overdosing on the Nembutal barbiturate she'd been taking. This, he knew, could shut down the diaphragm muscles that enabled her to breathe, so he counted her pills, saw she'd taken too many, and immediately phoned for help.

An ambulance crew arrived within minutes and revived Maril, who, once she was fully awake, realized how close she'd come to death. Miller believed the overdose was accidental, but the incident also showed the depths of her grief over the loss of her pregnancy—and the danger of the medication she took to numb her pain.

* * *

Maril flew from New York to LA in early July 1958, a month before shooting was scheduled to start on *Some Like It Hot*, her second motion picture with director Billy Wilder. By now, Maril's business partnership with Milton H. Greene had dissolved (but not their friendship) and Marilyn Monroe Productions was a thing of the past. So, embarking on a project produced by the Mirisch Company, she was again working within the studio system. Looking forward to reuniting with Mr. Wilder, she arrived happy, relaxed, and eager to start work. Not only had Billy been kind and understanding during her breakup with Joe DiMaggio, their previous picture together, *The Seven Year Itch*, was a huge hit.

16: THE FAMILY BUSINESS

GROWING UP, I WAS surrounded by people in the motion picture industry. Not just Dad and Mom and Nana and Aunt Effie but also members of our extended family. My uncle Daniel Sacks headed the film editing lab at MGM and worked closely, as well as uncredited, with his friend director David Lean on such films as *The Bridge on the River Kwai* (1957) (editor Sati Tooray would also go uncredited) and *Doctor Zhivago* (1965) (editor John Grover would go uncredited as well).

Danny was considered one of the best color editors in the business. He was the only one David Lean would trust when he was doing color. He could bring color out of stuff that nobody else could. Uncle Danny had been on the submarine that sat on the bottom of Tokyo Bay during World War II. This was done to escape from the Japanese.[39] He was over six feet tall and was probably banging his head on the ceiling.

Then there was Daddy's cousin Jack Warren, who had a long career in feature films and television, working primarily with Alfred Hitchcock and Cecil B. DeMille. Oscar-nominated for his black-and-white cinematography on *The Country Girl* with Bing Crosby and Grace Kelly in 1954, Uncle Jack also handled the color photography on *The Ten Commandments* a couple of years later.

Johnny added, "My dad was a very busy guy and didn't have a whole lot of time for me, but I loved him. He worked for Paramount for years. When I was a teenager, I reshot *The Ten Commandments* for fun… At Universal, my dad was one of Hitchcock's cinematographers. He was very close to Hitchcock and DeMille. As a child, I remember meeting Mr. DeMille a few times. He was an interesting, powerful man.

"At Paramount, I watched dailies for *Samson and Delilah* (1949) with my dad. Victor Mature was supposed to have this terrible fear of lions, and it was a blind lion called Jackie who was on cue. She would know how to growl and Victor was so afraid. On the screen, Mr. DeMille's screaming, 'Goddamn it! Get yourself out there and fight!' Later, Mr. DeMille came over to me and said, 'Johnny, I'm sorry if I used a little bit of rough language, but there are hard days like that.'

"Years later, Mr. DeMille said, 'You know, your dad is a terrible liar. He had me climbing this scaffold in Egypt scouting locations he was going to shoot, and he kept making me wait every couple of minutes at different levels.' It was because Mr. DeMille wanted to climb right on up to the top with his heart condition! My dad was saying, 'Come over here for a while and check this out.' He did that to save Mr. DeMille's life …

"One time, I went over to Jane Wyman's dressing room and she said, 'Johnny! I haven't seen you for a couple years! Come here!' We had a great visit, and she was just such a sweetheart."

My cousin Anne, meanwhile, danced under the name Anne D'Aubery in every Elvis Presley movie—including *Viva Las Vegas* (1964) with Ann-Margret—and other films such as *The Music Man* (1962), *Bye Bye Birdie* (1963), *The Nutty Professor* (1963), *Robin and the 7 Hoods* (1964), and *My Fair Lady* (1964).

And as if all that wasn't enough, at the age of sixteen I attended Hollywood High with several future TV and film stars: Mike Farrell (*M*A*S*H*), Stefanie Powers (*Hart to Hart*), Yvette Mimieux (*The Time Machine*), Linda Evans (*Dynasty*), and Ozzie and Harriet's boys, Ricky and David Nelson.

Sixteen-year-old Terry Karger (From the collection of Terry Karger)

I myself wasn't interested in going into show business. And I wasn't attracted to the boys who wanted to be actors. Instead, my first boyfriend, in 1958, was Walt Lewis, named after his father's boss Walter Annenberg, who'd created *TV Guide* five years earlier. The son of a Paramount publicity exec, Walt had already graduated high school and, while aiming for a law career, had a job making deliveries for a store called Liquor Locker on Sunset Boulevard.

Although living with my mom at the house on Selma Avenue, one summer night during the first two weeks in July 1958, before Maril began filming *Some Like It Hot*, I was at Nana's Voltaire Apartments home when I decided to play a prank on my boyfriend—one that I couldn't pull off by myself. So I had Nana call Liquor Locker and order two bottles of Dom Pérignon pink champagne. Then I waited, listening at Nana's front door for the elevator and Walt's footsteps in the hallway. Finally he arrived—and was surprised to be greeted by his girlfriend saying, "Come on in, Walt."

His second surprise of the evening: Marilyn Monroe stepping out of the kitchen to coo in her soft, sultry voice: "Well *hello*, Walter. I see you've brought my favorite champagne. How *thoughtful*."

Walt nearly dropped both bottles on the floor.

Maril and I laughed while Walt stammered and turned red. Then we all chatted for a while—with my boyfriend seated uncomfortably between Maril and me on the sofa. We knew we couldn't keep him there very long—he was on the job, it was nighttime, and we didn't want to get him in trouble. But he was predictably curious about how long I'd known Marilyn Monroe. So she answered for me:

"Terry and I have known each other since she was six years old. There's one thing I've never told her and this seems like a good time, now that her boyfriend's here...I've always been a little envious of Terry's legs."

"*You're* envious of *her* legs?" Walt asked incredulously.

I punched him in the arm with my fist.

Walt later told me he was amazed at how sweet, kind, and unassuming Maril was. She didn't come across as a major Hollywood star; instead, she was funny, giggly, and very much the girl next door— albeit one who was incredibly beautiful.

"Marilyn was very attractive, but I never thought she was Freddie's type," Walt remarked. "Freddie liked tough women: Terry's mom Patti was a hard, strong attorney; my mom Ruth, who once dated Freddie, was pretty strong and aggressive; and Jane Wyman was really tough. These were all women who dated or married Freddie Karger—a suave, great-looking guy."

It was good to have Maril back in Hollywood; I'd missed her terribly since her move to New York. When visiting the West Coast from time to time, she'd always show up at Nana's place. After Walt left for the evening, I was talking to Maril about going somewhere with one of my girlfriends. "It's great to have girlfriends you can do things with," she said. "I don't have many girlfriends besides your mom and your Aunt Mary. I don't know why, I just don't. I'm glad you do."

I often had the feeling that, even in her happiest times, there was a sense of wistfulness and almost a sadness about Maril. During those later years, her happiness always seemed a little off-key. She rarely seemed happy through and through.

But when Maril visited Nana again in late July, days after her visit with Walt Lewis and me, she seemed happy, almost giddy, because she was certain she was pregnant again and this time everything appeared to be normal. At this time, I mentioned to Maril again what I had told her as a child, that I wanted to be a teacher and she was elated. Although my parents had actively tried to dissuade me from pursuing a showbiz career, they needn't have bothered. I knew I wasn't cut out to be a performer—I'm too shy.

"I can't think of a more important job in the world," Maril replied. "Children need teachers they can look up to. Just be the person you were meant to be, T.K. Looks will get you far, but not as far as a good education."

Maril once told me her biggest regret was never finishing high school—which is why books were important to her. She always had them wherever she went and never missed an opportunity to ask what I was reading—while showing me the book she was carrying around. During this visit, it was *Life Among the Savages*, a collection of essays by Shirley Jackson about her adventures as the mother of little children—a choice that spoke to Maril's plans and hopes for her own life as a mother, now that she was pregnant again.

"I've always liked talking to you, T.K., ever since you were little," she said. "Remember when I used to drive you to Sunday school? Those were good times. I miss those days—but I also like watching you grow up."

Gossip columnist Louella Parsons reported the pregnancy news a month late on August 18 after weeks of denial by Maril and Arthur, who wanted to keep the pregnancy a secret, "Eight months from now, Marilyn Monroe's fondest wish will come true. She will have a baby. Tests have proved conclusively that the most publicized actress in the world is pregnant."[40]

Might another long-held dream be about to come true?

17: SOME LIKE IT HOT

PRODUCTION FOR *SOME LIKE IT HOT* began on August 4, 1958. At first Billy Wilder was pleasantly surprised by Maril's behavior on the set. After shooting an opening scene she felt didn't work, she suggested having her character, Sugar Kane, make her grand entrance at a train station; as the train is about to pull out, Sugar's derriere is blasted with a puff of steam and she stumbles into the members of an all-girl band.

Wilder went along with Maril's suggestion, and the result was a classic scene that serves as a charming introduction to the Sugar Kane character.

During the first few days of shooting, Maril arrived on time, was cooperative, and knew her lines. Very quickly, however, she slipped back into some bad habits: turning up late on set and forgetting her lines, forcing costars Jack Lemmon and Tony Curtis to do as many as eighty-three takes under hot lights, caked in women's makeup while strutting around in dresses and high heels.

In June 2014, I ran into Jack's son, Chris Lemmon, at the Laguna Playhouse. He was performing an uncanny impression of his dad—and reenacting touching moments from their father-son relation-ship—in the play he'd written as a tribute, *Jack Lemmon Returns*. Having known Chris since we were children, I met him backstage after the show, we talked about old times playing on the beach, and I showed him a photo of our dads together. Chris then recalled Jack mentioning how, during the production of *Some Like it Hot*, Marilyn's dialogue had to be written on cue cards and placed outside camera range.

When Nana, Mom, and I visited with Maril in the fall of 1958, she said she was having trouble concentrating while filming *Some Like It Hot*. This, she thought, was due to her being focused on having the baby and seeing the pregnancy through to delivery.

Yet even when she'd worked hard and knew her lines at the start of her career, chronic stage fright had always made it difficult for her to leave her dressing room on time.

In my opinion, the confidence and courage my father tried instilling in her was subsequently eroded by drama coaches Natasha Lytess and the Strasbergs; they wanted to ensure she remained dependent on them. Meanwhile, the Nembutal and alcohol she consumed not only affected her memory and made her undependable, they also did little to diminish her stage fright and insecurity. What a miracle the pills and alcohol didn't ruin the magic she was able to summon for the camera lens.

The filming of *Some Like It Hot* wrapped on November 12, 1958, weeks behind schedule and well over budget—almost entirely due to Maril's tardiness, no-shows, and endless retakes. Nevertheless, following its New York premiere on March 29, 1959, the movie was an instant hit with critics and audiences, grossing a then-impressive $14 million in the US alone. Forty-one years later, it would be voted number one on the American Film Institute's list of the "100 Funniest American Movies of All Time."

It's amazing that such a troubled production resulted in a motion picture classic. Once her work on the film was over, she spent several days resting at the Beverly Hills Hotel where Nana visited her in her luxury bungalow. Then, to minimize stress on her unborn baby, she was transported by ambulance to the airport for her flight back to New York.

On December 16, Nana received a call from Maril—and was in tears by the time she hung up the phone.

"What's wrong?" I asked.

"Maril lost the baby," she replied. "It's so *sad*, Terry. I told her she could try again. I told her to pray and everything would be all right."

Life, for Maril, was not going to be all right. It was going to get a lot worse.

18: THE MISFITS

My cousin Ben shared a story that took place in 1959, a few years after his mother and stepfather had moved to Little Silver, near Fort Monmouth, New Jersey. Maril was visiting their home, so Ben invited his best buddy Alan Peterson to join them. Alan and Maril, you see, had met three years earlier at a family gathering captured on 16 mm film by Ben's stepfather.

"Alan was the dance captain in the road company for the stage version of *West Side Story*," Ben explains. "He sat on the floor across the room from Marilyn and was thrilled to see her again. Then, all of a sudden, we heard a fire engine pull up in front of our house. Somebody had found out Marilyn was there and sent a false alarm so the firemen would come over and meet her. When she saw what was happening, she was beautifully gracious, went outside, signed autographs, and took pictures with them. She had a great time."

* * *

As a schoolgirl, Maril's hero had been Abraham Lincoln, and for many years she'd treasured a framed engraving of him. In 1951, during her first sit-down conversation with Arthur Miller at a Hollywood cocktail party, Maril had told him how much she admired the sixteenth US president. He, in return, had asked if she'd ever read poet Carl Sandburg's two-volume biography, *Abraham Lincoln: The Prairie Years*, and its Pulitzer Prize–winning four-volume sequel, *The War Years*. She hadn't—and she'd never even heard of Carl Sandburg, but she imme-diately bought all six volumes.[41]

Maril and Carl Sandburg met briefly on the set of *Some Like It Hot* in 1958.[42] Then, in 1960, when Sandburg was working (with-out credit) on the screenplay for *The Greatest Story Ever Told* and Maril was filming the romantic comedy *Let's Make Love* with Yves Montand, Sandburg was assigned an office near Maril's dressing room at Twentieth Century-Fox.[43]

"Marilyn had a mind out of the ordinary for show people," Carl Sandburg would recall. "I found her fairly well read. I gave her a book of my complete poetry. I wanted her to have it... She was not the usual movie idol. There was something democratic about her. Why, she was the type who would join in and wash the supper dishes even if you didn't ask her. She would have interested me even if she had no record as a great actress."[44]

Maril and Sandburg met several times after that, most famously in the New York apartment of his photographer friend Len Steckler. It was Steckler who took photos of the two of them at that late-De-cember 1961 meeting where Marilyn wore chic tinted glasses and had her hair dyed platinum white to match Carl's.

**Carl Sandburg and Gregory D'Alessio playing their guitars
on October 13, 1952 by William Arthur Smith**

"My apartment was near Central Park on 33 West 67th," Steckler would explain. "I met Carl through the Classic Guitar Society. He already knew my friend Gregory D'Alessio, a painter who brought me into the society. All three of us used to get together whenever Carl was in New York. We were often accompanied by our wives and several other people. Carl never told me when or where he met Marilyn. He didn't talk about things like that. Carl was always in the present.

"When Marilyn arrived, she greeted me, then rushed over to give Carl a big hug. Carl liked women and he had a playful side, but I never felt it was serious flirting. Carl had an ego, and young women like Marilyn reinforced it.

"I took plenty of pictures of Marilyn and Carl in my apartment. She was beautiful and charming, yet she seemed vulnerable. Marilyn sat next to Carl as he sang and played the guitar. He was not very good at it. His ability to play classical tunes was limited, but he knew how to play ditties like 'Goober Peas.'

Marilyn Monroe and Carl Sandburg by Len Steckler in late December 1961

"We eventually moved over to Arnold Newman's apartment. He lived in the same building, and his wife was there. People were coming and going all evening, and everybody drank a lot of Jack Daniel's, but I didn't drink anything. Carl and Marilyn danced, then they sat together and talked the night away. I don't remember when the party at Arnold's ended, but I know it continued late into the night after I went home."

Maril and Sandburg met again on January 20, 1962, in the Los Angeles home of *Something's Got to Give* producer Henry T. Weinstein. This was photographed by Steckler's friend Arnold Newman, who captured Maril wearing a dark scarf over loose, flyaway hair—without sunglasses.

Marilyn Monroe and Carl Sandburg by Arnold Newman on January 20, 1962

* * *

Marilyn Monroe had a sixteen-year career as an actress, beginning with a bit part as Evie the waitress in *Dangerous Years* (1947) and ending with her role as Ellen Arden in the unfinished bedroom farce *Something's Got to Give*—a remake of the 1940 screwball classic *My Favorite Wife*—opposite Dean Martin. Overall, she completed twenty-nine films and was partway through her thirtieth when she died.

During the first half of that sixteen-year career, she made twenty-three films. There were major roles in minor films (such as *Ladies of the Chorus* and *Don't Bother to Knock*) and modest roles in major films (such as *The Asphalt Jungle* and *All About Eve*). Even though movies like *Niagara* and *Gentlemen Prefer Blondes* made her a star, they didn't establish her reputation as a serious actress.

In the second half of her career, she only made six films. Two—
Let's Make Love and *The Prince and the Showgirl*—were underappre-
ciated, even though Marilyn delivered great performances in both.
The rest—*The Seven Year Itch*, *Bus Stop*, *Some Like It Hot*, and *The
Misfits*—are acknowledged masterpieces. It's a body of work worthy
of a reputation as a serious artist.

* * *

In July 1960, the Democratic Party held its national convention in Los
Angeles. My father and his orchestra were booked by the Democratic
National Committee to perform at a convention ball. Yet when he
learned John F. Kennedy was going to be the party's standard-bearer,
Daddy canceled his orchestra's appearance. No way did he want to
perform for the man who, he'd heard, was having an affair with Maril.

Caring very much about Maril as a friend, my father was well aware
of her vulnerability and resented anyone hurting her. So, informed
that Senator Kennedy was taking cruel and selfish advantage of her,
he was concerned the affair would eventually cause her serious harm.

Late July, meanwhile, also saw the start of filming in Nevada for
The Misfits, a powerful drama written by Arthur Miller and directed
by John Huston. Not only would it be the last completed film by both
Maril and costar Clark Gable, Arthur Miller wrote the part of Roslyn
Tabor especially for her, ensuring the personality mirrored Maril's in
several important ways.

As *The Misfits* told the story of a recently divorced woman falling
in love with an aging cowboy, it uncomfortably echoed real life for
Monroe and Miller amid their crumbling marriage. Her love of animals and aversion to their suffering was at the heart of his screenplay.

Roslyn meets Gable's character, Gaylord "Gay" Langland, when
she feeds some of her lunch to his dog and they strike up a conversation. Later, when Gay plans to hunt the rabbits that have been eating
the vegetable garden they planted together, he and Roslyn argue. At a
rodeo, she is angered when she sees horses and bulls mistreated, and
she declares (exactly as Maril would have done) that rodeos should be

banned. In a pivotal scene, Roslyn screams at Gay when she learns of his plans to sell captured wild mustangs to be slaughtered for dog food.

Production of *The Misfits* wrapped on November 4, 1960. Two days later, Clark Gable suffered a heart attack and died on November 16. He'd been Maril's movie idol when she was growing up; living at the Los Angeles Orphans Home, she hung a picture of him on the wall and told people he was her father. So finally working with "the King of Hollywood" had been a dream come true—especially as, throughout production, Gable had treated her with fatherly protection, even tolerating her late arrivals without complaint.

Gable's death came as a terrible shock for Maril. After returning to New York, she was awakened by a 4:00 a.m. phone call from a reporter callously telling her Gable had died. He wanted to get her reaction to the news, but she refused to make a statement. One of the first people she called and wept to was Joe DiMaggio.

After *The Misfits* was released, Maril told George Barris, "Some people like it, but not me. I was disappointed. The director, John Huston, he sort of fancied himself a writer, and he changed it from the original intention of Arthur Miller. Now, this director also did *Asphalt Jungle*, but he didn't fool around with the script. I personally preferred the script be left as the writer did it. Mr. Miller at his best is a great writer."[45]

Maril was always generous in her praise of ex-husbands DiMaggio and Miller. She endured a lot of emotional upheaval during the making of that film, so those emotions may have colored her view of it. Regardless, many critics and movie historians have asserted that *The Misfits* contains some of the finest dramatic work of Marilyn Monroe's career.

* * *

Just days after the end of production, Maril's publicist Pat Newcomb announced that the Miller marriage was over. Then, when Maril returned to New York on November 11, she called nationally syndicated columnist Earl Wilson and gave him an exclusive. In his next column, Wilson reported, "There will be a friendly divorce."

There were no children involved, no financial disputes. As usual, Maril just wanted to move on. And there to quickly fill the emptiness in her heart was Joe DiMaggio. Maril felt she could lean on him, and that was okay with Joe, who, by now, had apparently dealt with his anger issues.

That same month, Frank Sinatra visited Maril in New York and gifted her a little white Maltese terrier for Christmas. Aware she was going through a rough time because of the divorce, he gave her that little dog for companionship. Thanks to Sinatra's rumored connections to the Mob, Maril named the pup Maf—short for Mafia—and it accompanied her everywhere, including a reunion with Nana at the Voltaire Apartments during the next return trip to California. Maril, who loved all animals, had a special fondness for dogs—so much so, Maf's doggie bed was an expensive white fur coat that Arthur Miller had given her early in their marriage.

"Dogs never bite me. Just humans," she once told her good friend Truman Capote—a sad but undeniably true commentary on Maril's experience with the human race.

* * *

On Tuesday, November 1, 1960, Senator John F. Kennedy was on the University of Southern California campus for the First-Time Voters Convocation. While there, addressing a huge outdoor audience in front of Bovard Tower, he gave a speech about the importance of young voters being involved in their democracy while distinguishing between the two political philosophies the candidates represented. Afterward, he waded into the crowd, smiling and shaking hands.

I was in the crowd that day, and not only did I manage to get close to him, the crowd pushed me *into* him. At that time I had no idea Maril was intimately involved with Senator Kennedy, but I do now think that, next to my father, he was probably the most handsome man with whom Maril ever had an affair.

Exactly one week after my encounter with JFK on the USC campus, Americans went to the polls and elected him the thirty-fifth president of the United States.

On January 20, 1961, Maril flew to Juárez, Mexico, to file for divorce from Arthur Miller. She chose the same day as Kennedy's inauguration, hoping to avoid being noticed by members of the press. Yet word somehow got out, and she was met there by a gaggle of reporters.

The Misfits was released on February 1. Critics loved it, while audiences stayed away. Maybe the public preferred to see Marilyn singing and dancing instead of exposing her raw, truthful emotions. In any case, the public rejected one of the most important and powerful motion pictures Maril ever made. It barely earned back the $4 million spent to film it.

"I saw *The Misfits* and I didn't like it very much, to tell you the truth," recalled Maril's *Bus Stop* costar Don Murray. "So much of Marilyn's psychological suffering came through in that film and made it very uncomfortable for her. I could see how my friend Montgomery Clift had physically deteriorated after his car accident."

This was a reference to how, since a May 1956 crash while driving away from a dinner party at the Beverly Hills home of Elizabeth Taylor, Clift's terrible facial injuries had made him dependent on alcohol and drugs for pain relief.

In April 1961, Maril returned to Hollywood and reconnected with old friends, including actor Peter Lawford and his wife Pat Kennedy Lawford, the president's sister. This coincided with Clark Gable's widow, Kay, issuing a statement to explain she'd been misquoted and that she had never blamed Marilyn Monroe for her husband's death. Kay learned she was pregnant while Gable was working on *The Misfits*, and on March 20 she had given birth to a boy she named John Clark Gable. Responding to an invitation, Maril visited Kay and the baby at the Gables' ranch in Encino on her own birthday, June 1, and was thrilled to hold little John Clark in her arms. She and Kay talked long into the night.

On June 12, Maril and a host of Hollywood stars—including Jack Benny, Ray Milland, and Fred Astaire—were on hand for John Clark's christening at Saint Cyril of Jerusalem Catholic Church. This was where my cousin Jacqui was married; the same priest, Father Lalor, officiated. Columnist Louella Parsons was the godmother.

Maril returned to New York on June 29. For months she'd been plagued with intermittent pain and nausea. Doctors soon concluded her gallbladder had to be removed, and following the surgery, she returned to California, taking up temporary residence at the Beverly Hills Hotel from August through early September 1961.

"The last time I saw Marilyn was the summer of 1961," my cousin Johnny Warren recalls. "She gave me a big hug. I was at Immaculate Heart College on Western Avenue, working on my music minor, and I came over to Auntie Ann's. That was at the Crescent Heights apartment on the corner near Schwab's.

"That same day, my girlfriend Louise wanted to come over when I was at Nana's, but her dad wouldn't let her. So Marilyn got on the phone with Louise, who later became my wife. Her father also chatted with Marilyn but still wouldn't let her go. He was very overprotective of his daughter.

"Marilyn talked about Arthur Miller and how much she loved live theater. She couldn't understand the fame that comes with film. I recall changes in Marilyn after she'd been working with Lee Strasberg. Her poise was different—her facial expressions and the way she spoke. She became more refined and focused on what she could do to improve her acting, to communicate her thoughts.

"Marilyn was a loving, kind, beautiful girl. She knew how to act, and she knew how to sing 'Diamonds Are a Girl's Best Friend' and really sell it. But deep down, she was very shy. She'd had a hard childhood and she needed a family, someone to love and someone to love her. That's all she ever wanted when she hugged me and kissed me as a child. I bless Marilyn. Maybe she's happier where she is. This world today would probably be very cruel to her.

"Marilyn was just an average person in that she didn't have an ego. I ran the camera department at Fox for about fourteen years. The custodians and the drivers all spoke highly of Marilyn. I'll never forget that. And I never once told them I knew her. The working people were really sorry she wasn't there anymore. They said, 'Oh, she was so sweet. She treated us like real people.' Here's this dear girl that we loved. I was right there years after she had passed on, but her existence was still very much felt.

"She wanted a child so desperately, somebody to be a part of her who she could love. I don't think she ever really understood her fame. She knew her fame was there, but she was too genuine somehow, and that didn't quite work in Hollywood. I remember the first time I met her, she held me and hugged me. She was such a loving person, you just felt good being with her.

"That last day, she gave me a big hug and kiss goodbye. I remember we took several great pictures of that meeting. Marilyn was very excited about life. I had a little Pentax camera, I was into photography, and Marilyn said, 'That's fine. Sure, go ahead. Take the pictures.'

"I took a picture of my Grandma Effie on one side, Auntie Ann on the other, and Marilyn with her arms around them.

Nana, Marilyn Monroe, and Aunt Effie during the summer of 1961
at Nana's Crescent Heights Apartment near the corner of Schwab's
(Photograph by Johnny Warren) (From the collection of Terry Karger)

"Then Mary's last husband, Lowell Race, took a picture of Marilyn and me.

Johnny Warren and Marilyn Monroe during the summer of 1961 at Nana's Crescent Heights Apartment near the corner of Schwab's (Photograph by Lowell Race) (From the collection of Terry Karger)

"There were almost a half a dozen pictures taken.

Marilyn Monroe, Mary, Uncle John, and Lowell Race during the summer of 1961 at Nana's Crescent Heights Apartment near the corner of Schwab's (Photograph by Johnny Warren) (From the collection of Terry Karger)

"Two were of Mary, Lowell, Uncle John, and Aunt Effie, along with Marilyn and Nana's pet Billy the Bird.

Aunt Effie, Nana holding Billy the Bird, Marilyn Monroe, Mary, Uncle John,
and Lowell Race during the summer of 1961 at Nana's
Crescent Heights Apartment near the corner of Schwab's
(Photograph by Johnny Warren) (From the collection of Terry Karger)

Effie, Nana holding Billy the Bird, Marilyn Monroe, Mary, Uncle John, and
Lowell Race during the summer of 1961 at Nana's
Crescent Heights Apartment near the corner of Schwab's
(Photograph by Johnny Warren) (From the collection of Terry Karger)

Billy eventually met his demise by flying into the refrigerator one
day when Nana left the door open and closed it by mistake. Present
during that visit, Marilyn was deeply dismayed. Still, she was a dear,
dear friend of our family, and we were very honored to be part of her
family, too."

19: THE LAST TIME I SAW MARIL

I WAS GETTING READY to begin my junior year at USC when Maril called to invite me for lunch at the Beverly Hills Hotel. We'd talked by phone in recent years when she was spending most of her time on the East Coast, but I hadn't seen her in months. She was young and so alive, it never occurred to me that, in less than a year, she'd be gone.

I knew Maril and Nana often talked by phone. My mother Patti and Aunt Mary also kept in touch by continuing to hang out with her when Maril had time. Looking forward to graduating in 1963, I hoped my life would slow down a bit after college so I could actually see more of her.

Maril met me in the hotel lobby, looking as cute as ever in pigtails, with light makeup. In fact, she'd lost weight and now looked much as she had in her twenties. (I didn't know this weight loss was the result of her recent gallbladder surgery.)

"I hope nobody will bother us," she said, giving me a big hug and kiss on the cheek. Then we went to lunch at the Polo Lounge.

Maril seemed happy—but she did share one complaint. Fame, she said, was a huge burden. She was happy to be successful, but she missed the days when she could go anywhere and do whatever she wanted without being mobbed by fans or hounded by photographers.

"Sometimes," she said, "I wish people would leave me alone. I wish I could just be myself and by myself."

We didn't talk about her divorce from Arthur Miller, but we did discuss her renewed friendship with Joe DiMaggio.

"Joe and I aren't getting back together," she confirmed, "but we're better friends now than when we were married. He's been kind to me in so many ways."

Maril wanted to hear all about my studies and ambitions, as well as if I was still dating Walt Lewis—which I was. She said she'd just visited Nana at the Voltaire, asked me how my cousins were doing… and, of course, asked about Daddy. So I told her:

"You know he married Jane again in March."

"I heard! I couldn't believe it."

"They had a small ceremony at a Catholic church in Newport Beach. Uncle John and I attended."

"Do you think they're happy together? I really want Freddie to be happy."

"I think so. They seem great."

Laughing wistfully, Maril looked away.

"What is it?" I asked.

"Oh, why did Jane get to marry Freddie *twice* and *I* never got to marry him *once*?"

* * *

In September 1961, Maril checked out of the Beverly Hills Hotel and moved into the Doheny Apartments at 882 North Doheny Drive, where she'd lived eight years earlier. This is where I visited Maril for the very last time—between September 1961 and the first month or so of 1962.

By then, she was settled in and the apartment was comfortable, with all her books on the shelves and her beautiful white piano. Introducing me to her little dog, Maf, she told me he was a gift from Frank Sinatra. To me, she appeared very happy.

Marilyn Monroe with her dog Maf by Eric Skipsey in 1961

Although she asked me about school and our family, we *didn't* talk about her secret affair with President Kennedy. Had she mentioned that, it would have been the only thing we talked about, because I would have demanded to know *everything*. Yet while she was alive, Mom and Nana didn't mention what they knew about her affairs with the Kennedy brothers. It was only after her passing that they said something to me and my family.

Maril was happy, I was happy, and there was no reason to suppose this might be the last time we'd meet. It saddens me that I can only remember impressions: her hug, her kiss on my cheek, the joy in her eyes, the sunlight slanting through the windows, the books on the shelves, the white piano, Maf lounging on the sofa …

Had I known how soon I would lose her, I would have tried to capture every moment and remember every word.

* * *

My husband William had known my mother Patti for years. Mom did legal work for his parents when they and other East Anaheim homeowners were victimized by a mortgage fraud scheme in 1960 or '61. Someone was taking out fraudulent second and third mortgages on homes and leaving the homeowners stuck with the monthly payments. Because this fraud was being perpetrated in several states and involved organized crime, Mom worked closely in the Southern California area with Attorney General Robert F. Kennedy to bring the criminals to justice.

Sometime during her fourteen-year friendship with my mom, Maril confided to Patti that she had been romantically involved with President John F. Kennedy—and later (closer to Maril's death) with the president's brother, Robert Kennedy.

* * *

In January 1962, Maril put down a deposit of $5,750 on a home at 12305 Fifth Helena Drive in the Brentwood section of West LA. Built in 1929, the tile-roofed single-story Spanish-style house had four bedrooms, three bathrooms, citrus trees, and a backyard swimming pool, all cloistered behind a privacy wall within a cul-de-sac. A set of four tiles on the front porch depicted a coat of arms with the legend *Cursum Perficio*—Latin for "I have finished my journey."

Maril had never previously owned her own home—and this one needed work to make it her dream home. At the close of escrow in February, she'd paid $77,500, putting down half in cash and taking out a mortgage for the rest. Then she made several trips to Mexico and returned with (or shipped) ceramic tiles, decorative masks, furniture, pottery, and tapestries.

Maril lived for several weeks in the Brentwood home without furniture or floor coverings—and called it her fortress. Never mind that one of the bathrooms didn't work. Her housekeeper and personal assistant, Eunice Murray, was helping her fix up the place and make it livable, and she had little Maf to keep her company.

She felt so safe in that house, I'm sure she never imagined she would die there. And I'm also glad I didn't get an opportunity to visit. No way would I want to visualize what happened within those walls.

20: SOMETHING'S GOT TO GIVE

MARIL AGREED TO MAKE *Something's Got to Give* as part of her contract with Twentieth Century-Fox. More than a year since she'd worked on *The Misfits*, she had slimmed down and looked much like she had in her twenties. Sure, she felt the project was a step backward artistically, but she hoped it would boost her career following the two box office disappointments that had followed *Some Like It Hot* in 1959. She needed a hit and, as moviegoers loved her comic talents, she was returning to what she knew worked.

In *Something's Got to Give*, Maril plays Ellen Arden, a wife and mother of two small children. Lost at sea and declared legally dead, she is rescued five years later and returns to discover that not only her children don't recognize her but also her husband has just remarried. Consequently, Nick (Dean Martin) finds himself wed to both women and is desperate to gently break the news to his current wife, Bianca (Cyd Charisse).

Production began on April 23, 1962, and was troubled from the start. Maril phoned producer Henry T. Weinstein to tell him she was staying home due to a raging fever and sinus infection she had contracted during a recent return trip from New York City. Informed of Maril's illness, director George Cukor decided to film scenes that didn't require her on the set. However, her sinusitis turned into bronchitis and she didn't show up to work for over a month, putting the production two weeks behind schedule.

Years later, when viewing the surviving footage from Maril's uncompleted film, I watched this thirty-six-year-old woman walking around, smiling at the camera, and I thought, "This is the absolute pinnacle of her beauty. She was never as beautiful as she was just before she died."

When I looked at the shots of Maril doing camera checks, I could tell that, despite having been photographed her entire adult life, she was still not comfortable doing it. I could see her insecurities coming out.

Not all the delays were Maril's fault. The shooting script was revised daily, and writer Walter Bernstein was delivering new pages to the set minutes before the scenes were to be shot, leaving little time for Maril, Dean Martin, and the other actors to memorize lines and rehearse their scenes. Given that Maril had enough trouble learning lines when she had weeks to study the script, how could she be expected to learn her part in minutes?

Something's Got to Give would be a prophetic title for one of the most famous movies never completed.

On May 19, Maril took time out from filming to appear at President Kennedy's televised birthday party at Madison Square Garden. This was a Democratic Party fundraiser, and the studio had granted her leave—before she had taken sick and put the production behind schedule. Cukor, Weinstein, and studio executives were therefore unhappy when Maril went ahead with her New York appearance instead of returning to work.

President Kennedy's brother-in-law Peter Lawford emceed the gala event and introduced Marilyn while the band started playing. The spotlight hit the stage—but no Marilyn. So Lawford brought out the next guest. Later, he introduced Marilyn again—and again Marilyn failed to appear. This running gag created a sense of suspense and expectation, so when Maril finally appeared in the spotlight (introduced by Lawford as "the late Marilyn Monroe") the crowd was thrilled—especially after she removed her fur coat to reveal a sparkling form-fitting dress.

I watched the event on TV at my apartment near USC, and it was a breathtaking moment. Maril sang "Happy Birthday, Mr. President" in a whispery and sultry way, then went into a rewritten version of Bob Hope's theme song, "Thanks for the Memories," singing, "Thanks, Mr. President, for all the things you've done, the battles that you've won…"

At the conclusion of Maril's show-stopping performance, President Kennedy responded, "Thank you. I can now retire from politics after having had 'Happy Birthday' sung to me in such a sweet, wholesome way."

Maril's gushing performance ignited rumors about an affair between her and the president. Kennedy must have realized that if the gossip got out of hand, it could turn into a politically ruinous scandal. And he was also aware that what he regarded as a fling between them was, through her eyes, a serious romance. So he put a stop to it by no longer returning her calls.

JFK's silence meant rejection and abandonment to Maril. Nothing, not even death, terrified her like being abandoned.

After returning from the president's birthday bash, Maril engaged in a publicity stunt inspired by the subway-grate shoot for *The Seven Year Itch*—and took it a step further for *Something's Got to Give*. Instead of showing her panties, Ellen Arden would show *everything*—swimming nude in the family pool to wind up Nick and, especially, his new wife.

Marilyn Monroe by Lawrence Schiller on the set of *Something's Got to Give* in 1962

Maril was supposed to film the scene in a body stocking to simulate nudity. Instead, she invited a group of photographers to come photograph her while she did the scene fully naked.

* * *

Friday, June 1, was Maril's thirty-sixth birthday. After a day of filming, the cast and crew celebrated with a party, complete with a cake. They all signed a hand-drawn birthday card featuring a caricature of Maril nude and hiding behind a towel, with the words "Happy Birthday (Suit)."

That evening, she attended a muscular dystrophy fundraiser at Dodger Stadium. No one knew it then, but it would be her last day as a working actress—and her final birthday. Three days later, Maril called producer Henry T. Weinstein to tell him her sinusitis had flared up again, she was running a temperature, and she couldn't come in to work. On Friday, June 8, after Weinstein conferred with George Cukor, they decided to fire Maril and replace her with another actress. Weinstein informed Maril through her agent that she had been dropped from *Something's Got to Give*. And the studio then unleashed a blitz of bad publicity against her.

Hurt and humiliated, Maril countered the studio's attacks with a series of interviews in major publications, including an extended interview with Richard Meryman of *Life* magazine. It would be the last interview published in her lifetime. Even though she was subsequently interviewed by George Barris in July, this wasn't released until 1995, more than thirty years after Maril's death; the Meryman interview appeared in *Life* on August 3, 1962, a day before her passing.

Meryman said she looked beautiful but troubled as they talked about fame. "When you're famous, you kind of run into human nature in a raw kind of way," Maril asserted. "It stirs up envy, fame does. People you run into feel that, well, who is she—who does she think she is, Marilyn Monroe? They feel fame gives them some kind of privilege to walk up to you and say anything to you, you know, of any kind of nature—and it won't hurt your feelings—like it's happening to your clothing."

Maril also talked about using her fame as a gift to make other people happy. "I realize some people want to see if you're real. The teenagers, the little kids, their faces light up—they say, 'Gee,' and they can't wait to tell their friends. And old people come up and say, 'Wait till I tell my wife.' You've changed their whole day."

Maril knew that her fame could vanish as quickly as it came, and she was prepared for this. "Fame will go by and, so long, I've had you, fame. If it goes by, I've always known it was fickle. So at least it's something I experienced, but that's not where I live."[46]

Richard Meryman conducted his first interview at Maril's home in Brentwood on July 4, 1962. Meryman would continue to interview her on July 5 and 7, seeing Maril one last time on July 9 to approve the full transcript. Decades later, Meryman recalled, "I went in with this tape recorder that I didn't know anything about. I was setting it up and Marilyn came in to help me. Allan Grant, who was a photographer for *Life* magazine, went separately [on July 7. Grant and Meryman did not cross paths on this date as they had different appointment times].

Marilyn Monroe by Allan Grant on July 7, 1962

"First, she wanted to show me the house. That also meant walking around outside. Marilyn showed me a room off the kitchen, between the garage and the house, the guest cottage. She said she was having it made into a place where if a friend was in trouble, they could come and stay.

"There was nothing in her main bedroom—just the bed with a mattress on a spring. I suppose there was a bureau, but I don't even remember that. Across the hall, there was another room and it was totally empty."

During one of Meryman's interviews, Maril was, he recalled, "tired and went out to see a doctor and came back full of energy. I think she was getting shots. She had two doctors, from what I understand, giving her whatever she wanted. Marilyn said it was a vitamin shot, but she never said which doctor it was.

"After that, she said, 'Let me put on a steak,' and she came back looking kind of forlorn, saying, 'We don't have any more food left in the refrigerator.' It was fairly late.

"The first interview was around four hours. The significant thing about the interview is it was a performance. Marilyn wasn't just sitting there talking naturally. Everything was a little bit high-key. She wasn't over the top. Whatever she said, it was strong. What she talked about, she talked about with passion.

"I thought her laugh was great. I was on the *qui vive* during the interview, trying to be smart and ask the right questions, and that laugh sort of broke that feeling. Marilyn had me give her questions in advance. A couple of times when I would ask her a question, she would give me a prepared answer that had nothing to do with the question. She was keyed up and super prepared.

"Before the interview, I met her press agent, Pat Newcomb, and had lunch with her. She sat in on all the interviews. Afterwards, Pat called to thank me. She liked the story. I think after a while, she realized I wasn't trying to waylay Marilyn so she cleared the piece.

"Part of the deal was that I had to have the tape transcribed overnight, and I had some poor woman who did that. Then the transcript was delivered to Marilyn, who read it that night. Marilyn sat there and read it very carefully and was very smart about it. She said, 'I need to have things to read.' So Marilyn read it that night, and then during the following interview, same deal.

"Marilyn kept the manuscript, and I came and picked it up the next day. She had rewritten something in the margin and it was terrific. The one thing she changed was what she had said about her stepchildren, which is very understandable. It was all very innocent. She was protecting herself every inch of the way.

"What's special about that interview is how Marilyn's talking on the page. There's a big difference in how writing sounds and how speaking sounds, and she got it speaking perfectly correct. I used her words. Those were absolutely her transcribed words.

"Marilyn was my first major celebrity interview. Behind the scenes, a managing editor got the piece and didn't care about Marilyn and didn't want to run it. The next week, the managing editor had a substitute, who was the news editor, and he ran it. Boy, are they glad they published it. She died the next day.

"When Marilyn said, 'Please don't make me a joke,' it was rather sad. I think she was very insecure. Even after all of that, she thought I might somehow shaft her... My interviewing technique was to say as little as possible and to let her talk. She said what she wanted to say. That was part of the secret of all that...to let the person draw their own portrait. And in the process, reveal themselves quite a bit."

* * *

After Fox fired Maril from *Something's Got to Give*, the studio executives considered several options for completing the film. Their first idea was to rewrite the script for another actress. They considered replacing Maril with Kim Novak or Shirley MacLaine but finally opted for Lee Remick.

When writer Arnold Schulman learned that Maril had been fired, he refused to revise the script out of loyalty to her. Likewise, Dean Martin, who had approval of his leading lady in his contract, refused to make the movie without her. So Fox brought in writers Hal Kanter and Jack Sher to write a new script around the footage of Maril that had already been shot. Since only half or less of her scenes had been filmed, this turned out to be an impossible assignment.

Finally, Twentieth Century-Fox struck a deal with Maril. Instead of being paid $100,000 per her current contract, on August 1 she would be rehired for a $1 million, two-picture deal: $500,000 for *Something's Got to Give* and $500,000 for the starring role in *What a Way to Go!* (Shirley MacLaine would subsequently replace her because Maril passed away.)

Fox had capitulated to Marilyn Monroe, and the filming of *Something's Got to Give* was scheduled to resume in October. Buoyed by this total success, she told Nana she couldn't have been happier.

* * *

My cousin Anne had married Cherrill Consoli in 1956 while Maril was in England making *The Prince and the Showgirl*. At that time, Maril had thoughtfully sent the newlyweds a gift from London: a set of ornate candleholders. Now, in July 1962, Cherrill's phone rang.

"This was two to three weeks before Marilyn died," he'd recall years later. "I was in my home in Van Nuys when I received a phone call. I picked it up and thought it was my wife Anne trying to imitate Marilyn, which she had done several times. Then, when Anne walked in the door, I knew it couldn't be her. So I turned the phone over to Anne, and it was indeed Marilyn Monroe.

"After a few minutes of chatting, Marilyn said she wanted us to go over to Anne's grandmother's apartment. We called her Nana; I went along. Nana and Effie were already at the house and their brother John Conley came later. That afternoon, Nana and Marilyn talked for quite a while. Marilyn had brought her dog Maf and arrived with her chauffeur Rudy [Kautzky]. She was very upset because her greatest disappointment was her miscarriages. She regretted that she could never have children.

"Marilyn talked about the past and how Joe DiMaggio could be so possessive and jealous and how intelligent Arthur Miller was. Marilyn was a very close friend of Nana and Anne's mother Mary. Marilyn wanted Mary to be her manager, but Mary didn't think it was a good idea.

"I walked away with the impression that Marilyn was a very troubled woman. After all the talk, Marilyn started to play the piano while Nana and Mary were singing songs."

* * *

Once the Richard Meryman–Marilyn Monroe interview in *Life* magazine hit the newsstands on Friday, August 3, Maril spoke on the phone with a number of friends who, to her great relief, all raved about what a wonderful article it was. Among them was Nana, who later said Maril sounded happy, even excited, during their last conversation. She had won her battle with the studio, her face was on the cover of *Life* and *Paris Match*, her career was once more moving forward, and she was fixing up and furnishing her new home.

After Maril passed away, Nana and Mom each told me about conversations they had with her, which convinced me Maril had affairs with two of the Kennedy brothers.

Maril confided to Nana she'd had affairs with President Kennedy and, weeks before her death, his brother, Attorney General Robert Kennedy.

Nana was terrified for Maril, fearing she was in way over her head. Nana's brother, John Conley, had known the Kennedy clan well, especially Joe, the family patriarch. As I mentioned earlier, my great-uncle John Conley, Nana's brother, was a good friend of JFK's father, Joe Kennedy. Uncle John grew up near the Kennedys, went to Harvard with Joe, attended Joe Kennedy's wedding to Rose Fitzgerald on October 7, 1914, and was a business partner with Joe for a while.

Uncle John said he, Joe, and a third man sold swampland to unsuspecting Florida buyers. He also told us he was the ghostwriter for some of Joe Kennedy's Harvard term papers. Ronald Kessler's biography of Joe Kennedy, *The Sins of the Father*, states that Joe Kennedy offered to let my uncle ghostwrite Joe's sports columns for the *Boston Globe*.[47]

Nana had heard Uncle John's stories about Joe's bootlegging, stock market manipulation, political payoffs, and underworld ties. The father of the Kennedy brothers had been relentless in pursuing and maintaining power. Would his sons be any different?

Nana said Maril was very happy on that phone call, like a giddy teenager in love who honestly expected to marry Bobby Kennedy, and said Maril had insisted she knew what she was doing. Nana could only beg her to be careful and promised to pray—because she feared the worst.

But Nana was definite: Maril did *not* sound like a young woman on the brink of suicide, so that is why she always wondered if indeed the worst *did* happen the very next day, the day Maril passed, and whether her death (not by Maril's own doing) was indeed somehow connected to her recent relationship with Bobby Kennedy. Nana cried for weeks.

21: BYE-BYE, BABY

On Sunday morning, August 5, I was in my apartment near the USC campus. I had the radio on, playing music, when an announcer interrupted with breaking news: Marilyn Monroe had been found dead in her home in the Brentwood section of West Los Angeles.

I sat down in total shock and thought, "This can't be true." It had been months since I'd seen her—and days since I'd spoken with her by phone when she was happy, optimistic, and looking forward to going back to work on *Something's Got to Give*.

Maril *dead?*

No way!

Refocusing on the radio, I noticed the announcer had been replaced by music. Had I heard correctly? Starting to cry, I reached for the phone and, hands shaking, called Daddy. Then I dialed Nana's number and heard her crying, too. Joe DiMaggio had already called her with the news.

Sometimes I think back to that terrible Sunday morning and think about how Maril's sweet soul departed this earth.

* * *

Joe DiMaggio was in San Francisco when he heard Marilyn had died. He immediately contacted his son, Joe Jr., who was at Camp Pendleton, and arranged to meet him.

Joe Jr. was stunned and shaken. He had called Maril on Saturday night, just hours before her death, to tell her he'd broken up with his fiancée Pamela Reis. Maril had been happy to hear this news because she didn't think Joe Jr. was ready for marriage and was glad the young man had come to the same conclusion.

Now, both Joes were shocked and in tears. After flying to Los Angeles and checking into a suite at the Miramar Hotel, Joe Sr. called Maril's half sister, Berniece Miracle, who asked him to make the funeral arrangements—which he then did with the help of Maril's former business manager, Inez Melson.

* * *

Before she died, Maril had been looking forward to a dinner party on Sunday night, August 5. Gloria Romanoff, widow of restaurateur Michael Romanoff, recalled Frank Sinatra arranging the dinner and Maril confirming she'd attend as Frank's guest.

"Marilyn was in a stew about what to wear," Gloria remembered. "The dinner was in honor of some mutual friends, a couple—a distinguished engineer from Hong Kong named King Yan Wu and his wife, Madame Sylvia Wu. They had come to Los Angeles in 1959, and Madame Wu opened a restaurant in Santa Monica that same year which became very popular with Hollywood stars. They wanted to see us all, so Sinatra said, 'Let's take them to dinner,' and he invited Marilyn."

Instead of enjoying Maril's company Sunday night, Gloria mourned her death. When informed how many pills Maril had purportedly swallowed (the equivalent of forty-seven Nembutals and seventeen chloral hydrates), she added, "You don't find it ludicrous of someone suggesting she swallowed *sixty-four* pills?"

After learning Maril's stomach was empty during the autopsy, a suspicious Mrs. Romanoff commented, "Where did sixty-four pills go? In the years when film stars were under contract to studios, to the exclusion sometimes of the families, which is amazing to me, the studios would compose a scenario they wanted published. Sometimes, it was at great variance with the death, I'll tell you. 'Marilyn's our property and she belongs to us and we'll call the shots.' It's called *business*."

In the wake of Maril's death, Frank Sinatra reclaimed Maf the Maltese terrier from her Brentwood house and gave the dog to his secretary, Gloria Lovell. I later heard Maf got loose one day, ran into the street, and was killed by a car.

* * *

As mentioned earlier, Joe DiMaggio had been golf buddies with my Aunt Mary. So when Maril died, Joe called Nana and invited her and Mary to the funeral.

Joe DiMaggio paid for Maril's casket and crypt and spent the evening before the funeral in the mortuary viewing room beside that casket. There until eleven at night, he sobbed and knelt in prayer.

The private funeral was held on Wednesday, August 8, at Westwood Village Memorial Park Cemetery. Joe gave specific instructions that Frank Sinatra, Sammy Davis Jr., Peter Lawford, and the Kennedys were not to be admitted. When Sinatra and Davis arrived with their security guards and tried to get in, they were rebuffed.

Joe kept the service very small. Nana and Mary were two of the tiny group of people permitted. You can see them in the funeral photos, one with Joe DiMaggio to the left of Nana:

(L) Mary and Nana (R) Nana to the right of Joe DiMaggio

Only thirty-one people attended Marilyn Monroe's funeral. The attendees were as follows: Joe DiMaggio; Joe DiMaggio Jr.; Maril's half sister Berniece Miracle; my aunt Mary Karger; my grandmother Ann "Nana" Karger; Maril's last drama coaches, Lee Strasberg and Paula Strasberg; Maril's psychiatrist Dr. Ralph Greenson, his wife Hildi Greenson, and their two children, Danny Greenson and Joan Greenson; Maril's close friend and masseur Ralph Roberts; her housekeeper Eunice Murray; publicist Pat Newcomb; hairdresser Pearl Porterfield; longtime friend and makeup man Allan "Whitey" Snyder, his then-wife Beverly Snyder, and their daughter Sherry Snyder; hairdresser Agnes Flanagan; attorney Aaron Frosch; mime Lotte Goslar; hairstylist Sydney Guilaroff; chauffeur Rudy Kautzky; Enid Knebelkamp (the sister of Maril's mother's best friend, Grace Atchinson McKee Goddard) and her husband Sam Knebelkamp; business manager Inez Melson and her husband Pat Melson; secretary May Reis; attorney Milton "Mickey" Rudin; Joe DiMaggio's best friend, George Solotaire; and chambermaid Florence Thomas. Maril's foster father Erwin "Doc" Goddard (married to Grace McKee until her death) and his third wife, Anna Alice Long Goddard, were invited to the funeral but did not attend.

The six pallbearers were: Whitey Snyder, Sydney Guilaroff, Allan Abbott, Ronald Hast, Leonard Krisminsky, and Clarence Pierce.

A nondenominational pastor gave a brief homily drawn from Psalm 139: "I will praise thee; for I am fearfully and wonderfully made: marvelous are thy works."

One of Maril's favorite songs, Judy Garland's recording of "Over the Rainbow," was played. Joe DiMaggio wept throughout the service and kissed Maril one last time before the casket was closed and then moved to the mausoleum. There, Maril's body was interred behind wreaths and flower sprays sent by Arthur Miller, Frank Sinatra, and Jack Benny. For twenty years, from 1962 until 1982, Joe would have red roses delivered more than once a week to the bud vase adorning her crypt.

According to Maril's half sister Berniece Miracle and niece Mona Rae Miracle, Joe and Maril were planning to remarry. Mona Rae recalled, "Berniece's heartbreak at handling Marilyn's funeral was ameliorated by the help Joe gave her with arrangements. 'They were going to remarry,' says Berniece. 'Marilyn was thinking ahead to that.' I know she was planning to remarry Joe; he really was the love of her life. They could have made it work... I do not subscribe to any of these suicide theories."[48]

Morris Engelberg, a close friend of Joe, recalled, "The date of their remarriage was set: August 8, 1962."[49] Instead of remarrying on that date, Joe laid his beloved Marilyn to rest.

* * *

I can't accept the official verdict that Maril committed suicide. All the friends (including Nana) who talked with her on Friday, August 3, the day before her death, said she was happy and optimistic.

The coroner found her stomach suspiciously empty of any residue from all the Nembutal capsules and chloral hydrate she supposedly swallowed, yet she had enough drugs in her blood to kill three people—too many to be an accident as the autopsy surgeon Dr. Thomas Noguchi noted.[50]

She also had more drugs in her system than the number of pills she had on hand, which means she couldn't have ended her own life through an oral overdose of sleeping pills, accident or otherwise.

"I don't believe Marilyn committed suicide," said Richard Meryman, the former *Life* magazine writer, adding this curious statement about Maril's psychiatrist: "After Marilyn died, Dr. Greenson contacted me and wanted copies of the *Life* photographs, which I thought was tasteless."

No one in our family believed the official verdict. My cousin Johnny said, "I don't think she committed suicide. I really don't."

His sister Jacqui recalled, "When Marilyn passed away, I was living in Oregon while my husband was getting his PhD in clinical psychology at the University of Portland. I was shocked to hear she had passed away. She was such a sensitive, wonderful human being. Of course, they tried to make it seem like a terrible accident, as if she had just overdosed.

"The day before she died, Aunt Ann had talked to Marilyn on the phone. Ann was a very loving person, like a mother to Marilyn. I remember Aunt Effie saying, 'There didn't seem to be a problem that day, so why would she kill herself?'"

"My family never thought it was suicide," cousin Ben added. "Nana spoke with Marilyn the day before she died and said that Marilyn sounded fine and upbeat, not down or depressed. I was on my way to summer camp for the California National Guard. I heard the news when I got to Camp Roberts. One of the men in my squad who had a portable radio yelled out, 'Marilyn Monroe is dead!' I said, 'That's not true! You must mean Vaughn Monroe!'—a popular singer at the time. But it was Marilyn. I think the thing was covered up. Whoever did it, I hope he rots in hell."

22: MARILYN MONROE WAS MURDERED

THE FOLLOWING CIA DOCUMENT dated August 3, 1962 (one day before Maril died), is an extraordinarily revealing piece of information about Maril's intentions to hold a press conference and expose dangerous government secrets along with her affairs with the Kennedy brothers, John and Robert. Maril noted all this in her red diary, which she referred to as her "diary of secrets":

> Wiretap of telephone conversation between reporter Dorothy Kilgallen and her close friend, Howard Rothberg (A); from wiretap of telephone conversation of Marilyn Monroe and Attorney General Robert Kennedy (B). Appraisal of Content: [REDACTED]
>
> 1. Rothberg discussed the apparent comeback of subject [Marilyn Monroe] with Kilgallen and the break up with the Kennedys. Rothberg told Kilgallen that she [Marilyn] was attending Hollywood parties hosted by the "inner circle" among Hollywood's elite and was becoming the talk of the town again. Rothberg indicated in so many words, that she had secrets to tell, no doubt arising from her trists [sic] with the President and the Attorney General. One such "secret" mentions the visit by the President at a secret air base for

the purpose of inspecting things from outer space. Kilgallen replied that she knew what might be the source of visit. In the mid-fifties Kilgallen learned of secret effort by US and UK governments to identify the origins of crashed spacecraft and dead bodies, from a British government official. Kilgallen believed the story may have come from the New Mexico story in the late forties. Kilgallen said that if the story is true, it would cause terrible embarrassment for Jack [Kennedy] and his plans to have NASA put men on the moon.

2. Subject [Marilyn Monroe] repeatedly called the Attorney General [Robert Kennedy] and complained about the way she was being ignored by the President [John Kennedy] and his brother.

3. Subject [Marilyn Monroe] threatened to hold a press conference and would <u>tell all</u>.

4. Subject [Marilyn Monroe] made references to "bases" in Cuba and knew of the President's plan to kill Castro.

5. Subject [Marilyn Monroe] made references to her "diary of secrets" and what the newspapers would do with such disclosures.

The document was signed by James Angleton, then chief of counterintelligence for the CIA, and was first published by Steven M. Greer, MD, in 1999 on page 455 of his book *Extraterrestrial Contact: The Evidence and Implications.*

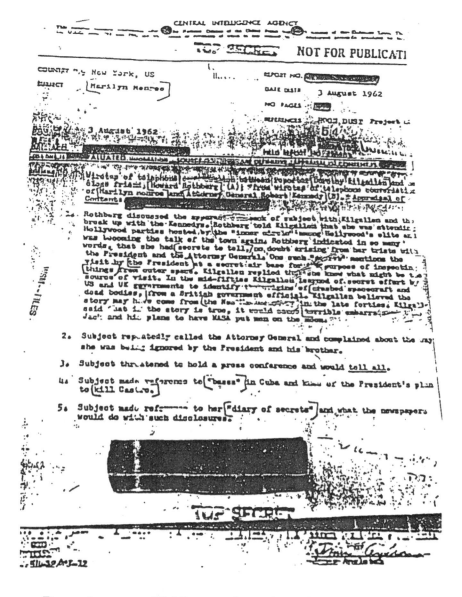

Dogged reporter Hal Jacques (coauthor of *Manson, Sinatra and Me*, 2015, and publicity consultant for Ted Charach's 1973 documentary *The Second Gun* on the RFK assassination) received a phone call on August 4, 1972, from an author. That same morning, the author had learned new details about Maril's last day alive on August 4, 1962, from a police contact. The author dictated to Jacques the police contact's words by reading a transcript of their recorded phone call. Jacques himself recorded the author's call and typed up his own transcript.

Robert Kennedy in March 1962 (MPI/Getty Images)

According to the transcript by Jacques, the police contact told the author: "RFK showed up at Marilyn's house. She had been bugging JFK and told RFK she would call the newspapers and tell them everything she knew about the Kennedys. You know how she would blow up. She became hysterical so RFK slapped her around to quiet her down. According to the LAPD investigational report, RFK and that actor Peter Lawford had indeed gone to Marilyn's house to see her on the day she died.

"In fact, Chief [Edward Michael] Davis (not Chief then) had gone to Washington, DC, to get a deposition from RFK. RFK told Davis about JFK's sexual involvement with Marilyn and Marilyn's embarrassing calls to JFK. RFK said JFK sent him to talk to her on Saturday, August 4, 1962. RFK and Lawford had taken a physician to Marilyn's house and she was given an injection of pentobarbital in an artery under her left armpit—it showed a tiny prick, and would you believe it, RFK signed and initialed every page of the deposition. The coroner had made a diagram showing where each and every needle mark went, all of which, of course, was left out from the final report. She also had several bruises on her—most, but not all, of which were edited out."

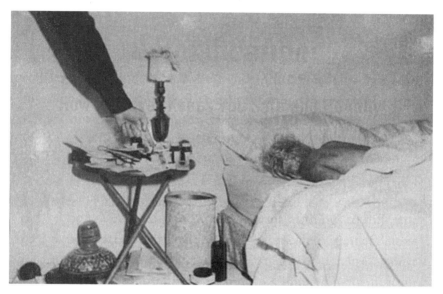

Police photo of a deceased Marilyn Monroe showing a bruise on her upper back not notated in the autopsy report

Per the transcript by Jacques, the police contact continued, "It was a big coverup and did not become a matter of public record. Her entire notebook [red diary, containing very dangerous and secret political information told to her by John and Robert Kennedy] was photographed days later by the LAPD."[51]

In 1978, an eyewitness LAPD detective, Mike Rothmiller from the Organized Crime Intelligence Division, saw a copy of Maril's red diary and Robert Kennedy's deposition in the top-secret OCID file rooms.[52]

The Marilyn Files Live Television Special Documentary, 1992

Maril's friend George Carpozi Jr. extensively interviewed Sidney B. Weinberg, MD, regarding his professional analysis of Marilyn Monroe's death and autopsy.

The Reporters Special Edition—Marilyn: A Case for Murder Television Documentary, 1988

Dr. Weinberg was the chief medical examiner for Suffolk County, New York, and he notated how Maril's toxicology reports "revealed a level of 4.5 mg. percent barbiturates [Nembutal] in the blood [equivalent to 47 Nembutals] and 8.0 mg. percent of chloral hydrate in the blood [equivalent to 17 chloral hydrates]. The liver contained 13 mg. percent of pentobarbital [Nembutal]. Since there are no findings of these drugs in the stomach and since numerous capsules and tablets of prescription drugs were found at the scene, all of the type, which are ingestible, it is difficult to conceive that some trace of these drugs would not be found in the stomach or intestinal tract.

"One might explain the lack of these findings in the stomach on the basis of an exceedingly long interval between the time the drugs were ingested and the time she expired, but in view of the levels in the blood and liver, this would not seem to be the case.

"The question is raised, did she take the drugs all at one time or did she take it over a period of hours? Again, we would expect to have some evidence in the stomach. The amount of drugs, such as barbiturates present in the stomach is also very important because it indicates intent to commit suicide. Naturally, the larger the amount, the more evidence for a suicidal intent and the quicker the death.

"This brings up another factor. The rate of absorption of the drugs from the stomach. The amount and kinds of foods and liquids in the stomach may delay or increase absorption of the drugs from the stomach into the blood stream. A description of the stomach contents estimated the volume to be no more than 20 cc ('the content is brownish mucoid fluid'), which is less than one ounce and that 'no residue of the pills is noted.' These findings are certainly not characteristic of an oral ingestion of large amounts of barbiturates.

"At this point, knowing the results of the toxicology examination and the negative findings in the stomach, one must seriously consider the possibility of an injection or the use of a suppository to account for the toxicology findings. In my opinion, it is unlikely that anyone could take allegedly 47 capsules of barbiturates [and 17 chloral hydrates] in seconds without having a trace of barbiturates in the stomach or in the first part of the small intestine. Although the death was certified as Acute Barbiturate Poisoning Due to Ingestion of Overdose, and although there is no question that the death was due to an overdose of barbiturates potentiated by the presence of chloral hydrate, there is no evidence to substantiate the mode of entrance of the drugs into the body was due to ingestion."[53]

Maril couldn't have swallowed the chloral hydrate in pill form without undissolved capsules showing up in her stomach, nor could she have been given a glass of water to drink that had been mixed with broken-down chloral hydrate pills.

The Marilyn Files **Live Television Special Documentary, 1992**

Schaefer Ambulance attendant James Hall would arrive later to the scene with his driver, Murray Liebowitz. After Maril's publicist, Pat Newcomb, had directed Hall and Liebowitz to the guest cottage where Maril was discovered unconscious, Newcomb told Hall, "I think she took some pills."

Hall then smelled Maril's mouth and noticed neither odor of drugs nor odor of pear (a fruity smell when chloral hydrate is orally ingested, the absence of which suggests that it wasn't swallowed in pill or liquid form). Hall also noticed there were no signs of vomit, uncommon among suicidal drug overdoses.

In 1982, my first boyfriend had heard about the reinvestigation into Maril's death. "I was a deputy district attorney for thirty-two years in LA County," Walt Lewis remembered. "The district attorney who handled the reinvestigation was Ron Carroll. Everybody called him Mike, but his real name was Ron. As I recall, Mike believed that Marilyn had committed suicide."

During Mr. Carroll's investigation, articles such as the following appeared in several media outlets, including the *Philadelphia Daily News*, on November 18, 1982:

"'Explosive' information claiming Marilyn Monroe was murdered by a doctor who injected a mystery fluid into her heart has forced further investigation of the star's death, authorities say. District Attorney Mike Carroll said yesterday that a story in the current issue of the *Globe* must be checked out before an investigation begun earlier this year into Monroe's death is complete. Twenty years ago, the death was ruled a drug overdose [probable] suicide.

"In the copyrighted story, headlined 'I Saw Marilyn Murdered,' a former [Schaefer] ambulance attendant James [Edwin] Hall claims he was reviving Monroe from a drug overdose when he was 'pushed aside by a "doctor" [positively identified by Hall as Dr. Ralph Greenson, Maril's psychiatrist] who [pulled out a needle from his medical bag, filled the syringe, and] injected a mysterious [brownish] fluid directly into her heart and quickly pronounced the actress dead.'"[54]

(L) Dr. Ralph Greenson from *The Missing Evidence: The Death of Marilyn Monroe* Documentary, 2014 (R) Schaefer Ambulance attendant James Hall's identikit of Dr. Greenson displayed in *The Marilyn Files* Live Television Special Documentary, 1992

James Hall recalled that the *Globe* newspaper "gave me six polygraphs and they hypnotized me twice. They regressed me and made me remember who the doctor was, what he looked like. Afterwards, when they brought me out of hypnotism, we did a police [identikit]. At that time, one of the [*Globe*] reporters walked by and he said, 'Hey, I know that guy!' and they pulled up the pictures of Marilyn's psychiatrist, Dr. Ralph Greenson, and that's who it was."[55]

Years later, in 1993, Murray Liebowitz, who validated he was James Hall's driver the night of August 4, 1962, would confirm to Donald Wolfe that James Hall's account of Ralph Greenson murdering Marilyn with the injection into her heart was accurate because Liebowitz said he had witnessed the heart injection alongside Hall. Hall asserts that, in addition to he and his driver Murray Liebowitz, RFK's brother-in-law Peter Lawford, Maril's publicist Pat Newcomb, and Sgt. Marvin Iannone were three other eyewitnesses to Ralph Greenson murdering Maril with the heart needle.[56]

(L) Murray Liebowitz (Courtesy of Sylvia Leib); (M) Pat Newcomb on August 5, 1962 (Foto File - Walter Fisher); (R) Peter Lawford (Weekend of July 27-29, 1962); (B) Sgt. Marvin D. Iannone on June 24, 1986 (Independent News Network)

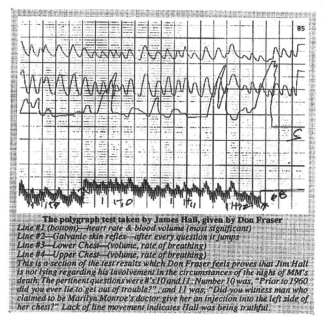

1992 polygraph test administered to James Hall by Don Fraser
from the University of Southern California as displayed in
the book *The Murder of Marilyn Monroe: Case Closed*

While there is no evidence to support that Maril died by a self-inflicted oral ingestion of drugs on an empty stomach, there is evidence to support the administration of a drug-laced enema (as opposed to a suppository) to Maril against her will, followed by a subsequent lethal injection to account for Maril's murder.

Peter Lawford's third wife, Deborah Gould, recalled Lawford telling her, "Marilyn took her last big enema." Not that Maril gave it to herself but that Lawford was aware how a drug enema would place her into a state of unconsciousness, accounting for much of the high toxicological findings of Nembutal and certainly all of the chloral hydrate.

Arnold Abrams, MD, said to author Donald Spoto, "The odds that she took pills and died from them are astronomically unlikely...I've never seen anything like this in an autopsy. There was something crazy going on in this woman's colon," since the coroner Dr. Thomas Noguchi had noted how "the colon showed marked congestion and purplish discoloration," which then-Deputy District Attorney John Miner, who also oversaw the autopsy, believed would have best been explained by the colon's contact with broken-down pills (Nembutal and chloral hydrate) mixed together in an enema.

Dr. Abrams denied the possibility that Maril could have given herself the drug enema, stating, "You don't know what the necessary fatal dose will be, and you have no guarantee that it's going to be absorbed before it's expelled. Look, if you're going to kill yourself with barbiturates, you do it with pills and glasses of water."[57]

Days after Maril's death, Maril's next-door neighbor at 12304 Fifth Helena Drive, Mrs. Mary W. Goodykoontz Barnes, would tell Sergeant Jack Clemmons, the first policeman officially at the scene, she had witnessed through her upstairs window Bobby Kennedy and a man in a suit with a medical bag entering Maril's house on August 4.

First Policeman on the Scene
JACK CLEMMONS

(L) Mary W. Goodykoontz Barnes (October 25, 1904–March 12, 1964) (University of Iowa yearbook dated 1927); (R) Sgt. Jack Clemmons in *The Reporters Special Edition—Marilyn: A Case for Murder* Television Documentary, 1988

This was during her regular Saturday afternoon bridge party with her friends, including Elizabeth Pollard, who was also an eyewitness to the attorney general's presence that day.

In addition to seeing Bobby Kennedy in the afternoon, Mrs. Barnes, Maril's housekeeper Mrs. Eunice Murray, and Maril's handyman Norman Jefferies (who was also Mrs. Murray's son-in-law) would later witness Kennedy again in the evening, this time accompanied by two men in suits, one carrying a medical bag.

Norman Jefferies and Eunice Murray on the morning of August 5, 1962 (Photo by Schulman-Sachs/Getty Images)

According to Norman Jefferies, during a time when Maril was clearly not in trouble from overdosing on sleeping pills, Kennedy along with his bodyguards, LAPD veteran partners Archie Case and James Ahern, had ordered him and Mrs. Murray out of the house—at which point Mrs. Murray and Jefferies walked the short distance next door to the house of Mrs. Barnes until Kennedy, Case, and Ahern left.

(L) LAPD Det. James John Ahern (From the collection of Anna Mae Benz);
(R) LAPD Det. Archibald "Archie" Bellamy Case
by Sgt. Conwell Keeler in 1948

Kennedy had initially returned to Maril's house during the evening, not to kill her but to simply find her red diary. Apparently, the Nembutal injections Kennedy had soon after instructed Case and Ahern to give her behind both knees and in the jugular vein in her neck would not suffice in subduing her.

"Give her something to calm her down" had been Kennedy's words caught over wiretap regarding the evening injections, as he placed a pillow over Maril's face to keep the neighbors from hearing her screams. She was still hysterical and wanted the three men out of her house. These injections had increased the level of Nembutal later found in her blood along with the injection in her left armpit from earlier in the afternoon.

Therefore, because of Maril's relentless yelling, Kennedy had ordered Case and Ahern to administer to Maril the drug-laced enema to knock her out. Now that she was unconscious, Kennedy was able to continue his search for Maril's red diary uninterrupted. After a thoroughly exhaustive search for the diary turned up nothing, Kennedy stepped out front with Case and Ahern to regroup.

Within minutes, after hearing Maril's white Maltese terrier Maf barking in the guest cottage, Eunice Murray and Norman Jefferies left the house of Mary W. Goodykoontz Barnes and decided to return to Maril's.

When Mrs. Murray and Norman Jefferies had discovered her, Maril was nude, unconscious, and facedown leaning on the phone. Against everybody's expectations, Mrs. Murray, according to Jefferies, called Schaefer Ambulance, which truly must have alarmed Kennedy, who was still at Maril's house out front and had not yet entered Peter Lawford's Lincoln Continental.

Immediately upon learning of the ambulance call, Kennedy would turn to Plan B, which was to have Maril killed. He couldn't afford for her to be saved within minutes of the ambulance's arrival if he couldn't find the diary. Unfortunately for Maril, nobody realized that shortly after calling the ambulance, Mrs. Murray had gone to Maril's main bedroom to place the infamous red diary in her basket of things to protect Maril's privacy, thereby unwittingly sealing her employer's fate.

The truth is Kennedy had already searched the main bedroom earlier in the day and discounted that location during his evening search. Before Maril had entered the guest cottage (to investigate the noise made by the forcible opening of one of her two filing cabinets by Kennedy, Case, and Ahern), she had been talking on the phone with her lover, Mexican screenwriter José Bolaños.

José Bolaños and Marilyn Monroe at the Golden Globes
on March 5, 1962 (Hulton Archive/Getty Images)

Bolaños did admit Maril had told him weeks before her death how she had "long, heated discussions" about Castro's Cuba with Robert Kennedy.[58] She very likely may have been dictating information to Bolaños from her red diary in her main bedroom—years later he would say of their last phone call that she had told him "something that will one day shock the whole world."[59]

On Monday morning, August 6, Norman Jefferies asserted he witnessed Mrs. Murray handing Maril's red diary and one of her address books to a driver for the Coroner's Office looking for Maril's next of kin.

As for the expelled enema, it had made a huge mess, soiling the bed in the guest cottage (Maril would later be moved to her main bedroom where she was discovered by police). However, when the ambulance arrived, Maril was found face *up* on the guest cottage bed (not facedown as Mrs. Murray and Norman Jefferies had discovered her) without a sheet or blanket as James Hall noted.

Maril must have been dried off and moved. Before the arrival of the ambulance, the soiled sheets were obviously taken away from the bed. What's more, the first officer at the scene, Sergeant Jack Clemmons, oddly noted Mrs. Murray operating the washing machine and the dryer when he arrived. She had been washing the soiled bed linens.

Back to the night of August 4, shortly after Mrs. Murray had called the ambulance upon discovering an unconscious Maril, a frantic Kennedy quickly set Plan B in motion by calling up Dr. Ralph Greenson, who lived less than one mile from Maril.

According to Peter Lawford, Kennedy had "convinced" Greenson over the phone that the psychiatrist's affair with Maril would *also* be exposed (which Kennedy knew wasn't true) along with her affairs with the president and the attorney general first thing Monday morning. Greenson assured Kennedy he would be right over.

Thus, Lawford concluded Robert Kennedy "set up" Greenson to "take care" of Maril. When Greenson arrived on the scene at Maril's house, Kennedy provided Greenson with a needle from Case and Ahern's medical bag. Kennedy instructed Greenson to play off the injection in front of any eyewitnesses as a failed adrenaline shot.

As it turned out, Greenson entered at the guest cottage with the heart needle in a medical bag mere *minutes* after Schaefer Ambulance attendant James Hall and his driver, Murray Liebowitz, had already placed a resuscitator on Maril, which was bringing her color back.

Next, Greenson suspiciously instructed the machine's removal, after which he pulled out a heart needle from his medical bag, filled the syringe with a "brownish fluid," and thrust the needle into her heart, a lethal undiluted pentobarbital injection. Maril died as a result, and now Plan B was complete. The Kennedy dynasty had been saved from ruin.

However, all of that was seemingly about to be undone just twenty-five minutes after Maril's murder. At 12:10 a.m. on August 5, 1962, Beverly Hills detective Lynn Franklin pulled over a drunk Peter Lawford at the intersection of Olympic and Robertson boulevards for speeding.

History's Mysteries: The Death of Marilyn Monroe
Documentary, A&E Television Networks, 2000

An agitated Robert Kennedy was in the backseat, and Maril's murderer Ralph Greenson sat silent in the front passenger seat. While Franklin had already been acquainted with Lawford and Kennedy, the detective would later assert he positively identified Greenson when he saw footage of Maril's funeral.

Franklin brought to Lawford's attention that he had been driving in the wrong direction if his intention was to head toward Los Angeles International Airport to drop off Kennedy (so he could return to San Francisco). As luck would have it for the three occupants in the Lincoln Continental sedan, Franklin said he issued a warning to Lawford since the attorney general was in the car.

Two years later, in 1964, *Something's Got to Give* photographer William Woodfield asked Ralph Greenson how Marilyn Monroe died over a recorded phone call. In 2010, Greenson's son Danny would confirm to Christopher Turner his father's voice on the recording. It's difficult *not* to think of James Hall's testimony of witnessing Greenson inject Maril in the heart when Ralph Greenson had told Woodfield, "I can't explain myself or defend myself without revealing things that I don't want to reveal. I feel I—I can't, you know—you can't draw a line and say, 'Well, I'll tell you this but I won't tell you that.' It's a terrible position to be in to have to say, 'I can't talk about it' because I can't tell the whole story... Listen, you know, talk to Bobby Kennedy."[60]

The autopsy surgeon, Dr. Thomas Noguchi, who ruled Maril's official cause of death a "probable suicide," would ominously state in 1968, "You see, the whole thing was treated as a non-homicide. The evidence had been disturbed." Noguchi would relay decades later that Coroner Theodore J. Curphey, M.D. had "certified the manner of death to be 'probable suicide,' but the office could not find necessary factors to state it as suicide."[61]

History's Mysteries: The Death of Marilyn Monroe
Documentary, A&E Television Networks, 2000

George Barris took the last professional photograph of Marilyn Monroe alive on July 13, 1962. Barris's daughter Caroline revealed: "The coroner Noguchi called me one day, trying to reach my father, and we were talking on the phone, and Noguchi said Marilyn Monroe was murdered and they made him say certain things and he told me straight out that it was a cover-up. He said it was really obvious she was murdered when they got her. And he said her face was beat up.

"Noguchi told me, 'It was very clear she was murdered. There were all these signs that she was murdered and there was nothing in her stomach because they put everything intravenously. If she took pills, it should be in her stomach. If you look at the pictures, the pill bottles are standing up straight, and it takes time to put the caps to the pill bottles back on. There would have been a mess, the pill bottles would've been open and on the floor.'

"These were all descriptions, Noguchi said, of somebody who covered up but didn't even do a good job. I remember we spoke on the phone for a long time. He said there was a lot of bruising and stuff on her face, and he was sure she had struggled, that she fought for her life, that it was no accident.

"My father told me the same story as Noguchi, that Marilyn was murdered. My dad just spoke with her the day before and that there was no way she would've taken her own life the next day. That's why, after Marilyn died, my father moved to France. There was too much heat. He was probably afraid for his life."

"Noguchi never believed it was suicide," concurred Raymond Strait, Jayne Mansfield's press secretary, "but they shut him up real quick. I knew Tom Noguchi. He said he never believed for a minute that she committed suicide. He wanted to blow the whole thing on Marilyn Monroe, but [his superiors] weren't having it."[62]

Joe DiMaggio went to his grave believing the Kennedys, specifically Robert Kennedy, murdered Maril. He told his close friend Dr. Rock Positano, "I always knew who killed her. She told me someone would do her in, but I kept quiet."[63]

Maril feared she would be killed. She also had a problem with drugs and alcohol. If it wasn't suicide, and it wasn't an accident, then it had to be a homicide, death at the hands of another human being. The killers chose a perfect murder weapon—a barbiturate overdose—that would make her death appear as a suicide or an accident.

On the "official report," Maril would have supposedly ingested sixty-four pills, yet no trace of these pills was found in her stomach during the autopsy. Not one undissolved capsule!

My mother Patti believed Maril was murdered and that there was a high-level cover-up of the crime in place. Mom shared her theory with some friends a few days after Maril died—and reported that, very soon after, she was nearly run off the road by a mysterious car.

Just recently, I went in for a checkup at the pain doctor's office, and this middle-aged nurse told me she knew a man who worked on the autopsy of Maril [then-Deputy District Attorney John Miner]. That man said he thought she didn't commit suicide, that Maril had been murdered.

The Reporters Special Edition—Marilyn: A Case for Murder Television Documentary, 1988

It makes me sad my Maril left too soon, not by her own doing, but by the doings of others.

May Maril finally know the peace that eluded her in life.

CODA

I DON'T THINK MARIL ever stopped loving my father. Whenever I visited with her, she'd ask about "Freddie" with a happy gleam in her eye. She had moved on and married Joe, then Arthur Miller. But I think her first true love, my dad, always had a special place in her heart.

At the time of Maril's passing, my father was in the middle of his second marriage to Jane Wyman. During an argument in October 1963, Jane walked out on Daddy. Their divorce was finalized on March 9, 1965.

"Jane and I love each other very much, and always will, but we can't live together," he once told me. And it was true. They remained friends—just as Daddy and Maril had remained friends until her death.

* * *

I graduated from the University of Southern California in 1963 with a major in education and a minor in English, then started teaching in November of that year—the same week President John F. Kennedy was assassinated. I taught at one of the best schools in the city, Crescent Heights Elementary; later, at Westwood Elementary, many of my students were the children of such TV and motion picture stars as Ronny Cox, Micky Dolenz, Millie Perkins, and Richard Pryor. At parent-teacher nights, I had some of the biggest stars in Hollywood sitting in those little desks. Living and working in Los Angeles, I was always surrounded by movie people.

I made a lot of friends in the teaching profession, but I never talked about my family background in show business and never mentioned growing up around Marilyn Monroe, Jane Wyman, and Ronald Reagan. Occasionally, friends and associates who visited my house and saw some of my photos would say, "Is that who I think it is?"

* * *

Only after seeing my life through the eyes of my friends did I realize what an unusual and special life I've had. I've learned to make my own opportunities. I'm an adventurous person. I got started at an early age. I always wanted my father to take me to Ocean Park Pier for my birthday to ride the roller coasters. I brought a couple of girlfriends with me. The girls were crying hysterically while I was just having the best time.

I enjoyed teaching very much, but I sometimes ask myself what it would have been like to attend the USC School of Cinema. I would not have wanted to act, because of my certain shyness, but I would've liked to have been involved in some way in the motion picture business. I guess it "runs in the family," but Daddy never encouraged it. I certainly am proud of all the special, talented people who surrounded me during my lifetime. Today, I'm still involved with many in show business.

Two years after the making of *Doctor Zhivago* (1965), Mom befriended a French woman named Flora, who was a dialect coach for French actresses making American films. One of those actresses was named Dany Saval, who starred in *Boeing Boeing* (1965) with Jerry Lewis and Tony Curtis. In 1972, Dany married one of France's most famous entertainment figures, Michel Drucker. My ex-husband and I were at their wedding in Las Vegas. They have three houses in France, and I've been to all three of them. One was in Paris, another in Normandy, and the other in Provence, which is in the south of France. My current husband William and I remain in touch with them, and we visit every couple of years. Dany also works with Brigitte Bardot saving animals as an animal rights activist.

* * *

In my spare time, I enjoy bike riding from Newport Beach to San Diego, and I've done that several times. Some of my adventures have included parasailing, riding the rapids on the Snake River, and jumping into that river from a fifty-foot suspension bridge. There was this other girl who jumped, too, and she was very big-breasted, so I can't imagine how that felt.

Traveling is one of my favorite things to do. One of my most memorable trips was as an educator. I love to meet people from other cultures. I was chosen by USC to go to a cultural exchange in Japan. We were guests of the Japanese government, and they took us all around the country. I went to different islands and was given a tour of the grounds of the Imperial Palace and inside the prime minister's residence, which was written up in a Japanese newspaper. I was one of a select group of teachers to go all over Japan learning the *soroban* (abacus), and it was one of the most memorable trips of my life. How truly lucky I have been, and I appreciate all the opportunities that I have had.

* * *

Daddy would often tell me how important it was to be a good citizen. He loved to give me little bits of advice like that throughout my life. From the time I was little, I was the apple of Daddy's eye. He always gave me a party for my birthday; I'd have my friends over and he'd play the piano and entertain. He loved to make people happy with his music, and my friends adored him.

The Love-Ins (1967) with music by Fred Karger

My father went on to write songs for Elvis Presley films like *Harum Scarum* (1965), *Frankie and Johnny* (1966), and *The Love-Ins* (1967) as well as some of the religious songs Elvis recorded, including 1967's "We Call on Him" (cowritten with Ben Weisman and Sid Wayne). I worked at Westwood Elementary until Dad died in 1979, and it now seems that everywhere I turn, I hear his music. I miss him, but his music reaches out to me across the years and helps me feel he's still with me.

Years ago, I went to Mexico with my girlfriend Hermine Hilton. She has had many careers, including consulting with Fortune 500 companies as "America's Memory Motivator." She wrote the lyrics to "You Can Count on Me" for Sammy Davis Jr. to record in the Netherlands for the theme song to the TV show *Hawaii Five-O*.

One evening while Hermine and I were in Mexico, we had too many tequilas. Feeling hung over the next day, I turned on the TV— and the 1959 movie *Gidget* was playing.

Gidget (1959) with music by Fred Karger

Daddy composed the music for the film, including the song "The Next Best Thing to Love," sung by James Darren (another one of Daddy's voice students). Hearing Daddy's music helped me through my hangover.

When William and I obtained our marriage license on September 13, 1997, we turned on the radio and heard my dad playing the piano from *Picnic* (1955) to the song of the same name. He wrote some of the cues. When they had that fabulous dance scene where Kim Novak comes down the steps, that's my dad playing the whole song. It was a very sensual dance sequence. I have a photo of Daddy with Kim Novak that was taken on the set.

Fred Karger and Kim Novak on the set of *Picnic* (1955)
(From the collection of Terry Karger)

Most notably, they worked together on *The Eddy Duchin Story* (1956), *Pal Joey* (1957), and *Bell, Book, and Candle* (1958). My dad had a stint with Kim Novak. He was hanging out with her for a while. They were dating after his first divorce with my stepmother Jane.

Years later, I was in Palm Springs with my girlfriend Dawn. She told me that the local TV station showed *I Love Lucy* reruns every afternoon. I said, "Really? My father wrote The Straw Hat song for Desi Arnaz. He performed it on *I Love Lucy*."

Dawn said, "Let's go see if *I Love Lucy* is on!"

We turned on the TV—and out of the 180 *I Love Lucy* episodes that were produced, the station was airing that very episode from season one, episode eight ("Men Are Messy"), and I got to watch Desi Arnaz perform my father's song in a dance scene with a cleaning lady. It was like a gift from Daddy.

The Straw Hat song was actually first played in a Desi Arnaz movie from Columbia Pictures called *Holiday in Havana* in 1950. I'm certain its appearance in *I Love Lucy* was a wink and a nod to the earlier picture.

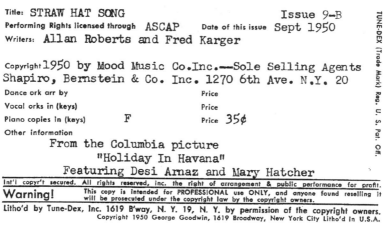

The Straw Hat Song (1950) (ASCAP) (From the collection of Terry Karger)

During the last years of his life, Daddy lived on Mandeville Canyon Road, west of UCLA. When he and I went out together, women would flirt with him. If they knew I was his daughter, they'd say, "Your father is so handsome!"

He called me almost every night when I was attending USC, and I always loved talking to him. When I began teaching, he'd come to my school and teach piano to the kids. He was funny and engaging, and he knew how to get children excited about music.

In the spring of 1979, he was still as handsome as ever, but he had begun to slow down. I'd offer to take him to lunch, and he'd say, "I think I'll stay home today. I'm not feeling a hundred percent."

As my birthday approached in 1979, he said, "Terry, I want to give you another party. Invite your friends. We'll have a great time."

"Maybe next year, Daddy," I replied. "This year I want to do something different. Don't make me feel guilty."

"Okay, Terry. Whatever you say."

I didn't know how sick he was. A few days later, he went into a coma, and on August 5, 1979—exactly seventeen years to the day that Maril was found dead—my father died of acute leukemia.

His best friend and longtime golfing buddy, Jack Lemmon, delivered Daddy's eulogy. It was a sweet and glowing tribute, and he closed by joking, "Now I can finally beat Freddie at golf."

My friend Vivien Atkin sat with me at the funeral, in the company of many of Daddy's longtime Hollywood friends. "That woman's familiar," Vivien whispered. "Who is she?"

"Rita Hayworth," I replied.

She and Daddy had been close for years. They often worked together on pictures at Columbia, such as *Gilda* (1946), and I'm surprised they didn't end up together.

Rita Hayworth with Fred Karger on March 14, 1952, on the set of
Affair in Trinidad **(The Silver Screen Archives) (Columbia Pictures)**

Rita Hayworth with Fred Karger on March 14, 1952, on the set
of *Affair in Trinidad* (Photo by Lippman) (Columbia Pictures)

After the service, several people told me my stepmother Jane Wyman had slipped in late, disguised behind big sunglasses, and then stepped out early. It had been fourteen years since her second divorce from Daddy, but they never stopped caring for each other.

"When Fred died, Mom went on to become a Third Order Dominican nun," says my stepbrother Michael. "In fact, she was buried as a Dominican nun. Historically, if you go back to the Catholic Church, spouses of deceased husbands went on to become nuns who worked in the hospitals, so my mom went on to become a nun."

Colleen and Michael Reagan by John M. Heller
on April 7, 2007 (Getty Images)

Today, Michael and I are close. He has a wonderful personality, a great family, and always has me laughing. Michael was telling us that one day a waiter spilled coffee on his lap. He asked the waiter, "Is this regular coffee or decaf, because I want to know if I'll be up all night!"

Another time, my husband and I were on a cruise with Michael and his wife Colleen. The four of us were having a lovely dinner when the maître d' came over and told Michael that a gentleman at another table said that he looked familiar and was trying to figure out who he was. Michael replied, "Tell him my father was president of the United States."

"When you have a parent that is so iconic in his time," Michael recalled, "because of what he had done, and who he was, it was hard not to get overshadowed. I think what it does, your self-esteem is not built up the way it should be because if you're a success, people say, 'The only reason you're a success is because of who your mother or father was.' If you're a failure, they say, 'You were a spoiled brat anyway. You should have been a failure.' So you never get that 'What have I accomplished?'

"At one time, I held five world titles in power-boat racing. I was inboard rookie-of-the-year. In 1966, I became world champion. In 1967, I set the five world records in racing for distance. In the 1980s, I did fundraisers for the Olympic Games. I've written several books and nobody knows that because my father was Ronald Reagan. It is very hard to be the son or the daughter of someone who was really, really famous.

"I tell people, I have this vision where I walk in and rob a bank, shoot and kill the tellers, and the police would be there to arrest me. Before he puts me in the back seat of the car, the officer would say, 'Your father was the greatest President we ever had. Can I get a photo with you? I brought my iPhone.' And I would say, 'I just killed six tellers and robbed a bank!' But, I mean, that's what you go through!

"I did talk radio for twenty-six years from 1983 to 2009, and these people listening in will send you little notes: 'Yesterday, you used incorrect grammar,' and you just go, 'Oh, please!' I did it. I enjoyed it and continue to speak all over the country. I do occasional television appearances. Also, I started an e-mail service called Reagan.com as a business venture.

"My wife Colleen owns a travel business, so she's always busy doing that, sending people all over the world, and we go, too. Terry and her husband often go with us."

* * *

Maril had an allure and an appeal few men could resist. Daddy certainly found her attractive, even though he felt he couldn't marry her. But I don't think she ever gave up wishing she could be the wife of Freddie Karger.

Had they married, how different would our lives have been? What would Marilyn Monroe's life have been like? Would she have avoided the destructive paths that led to her death at age thirty-six? Could she have overcome her anxieties, her terrors, her tormented memories, and her fear of abandonment? Daddy always tried to build her confidence and help her face life on her own terms. Maybe he could have helped her find the inner strength to live free of pills and alcohol.

My father did help Maril find her voice and develop the artistry she needed to succeed as a performer. She had other teachers and coaches who helped manifest her talent, but my father laid the foundation and made everything else possible. Her drama coaches, Natasha Lytess and the Strasbergs, made her feel weak and needy, but Daddy assisted her to find her strength.

Some people seem to think Maril's untimely death made her a legend by preventing her from outliving her youthful beauty and sex appeal. As one writer observed, Marilyn became "the ageless, ever alluring sex siren flash-frozen in time."[64] But those of us who knew Maril as a friend and family member don't think of her as "flash-frozen in time." We think of her as a beautiful soul we miss dearly and will never see again in this life.

I believe she would have been an even greater legend had she lived. So many wonderful actresses have aged gracefully through their forties, fifties, and beyond: Meryl Streep, Sigourney Weaver, Helen Mirren, Jane Fonda. In my opinion, Maril could have been one of them, but I also wished, by that time, she would have at least overcome her insecurities and satisfied her hunger for love.

If only she had lived long enough to absorb more of Nana's motherly wisdom. I can picture an older, wiser Maril, with her loving heart, her sweet and generous spirit, sharing that wisdom with young starlets, saving them from the same mistakes she had made. She could have lived to become a Nana-like mentor to young women with ambitions of stardom.

I can easily picture Maril—the young woman who drove me to Sunday school and took me to Wil Wright's ice cream parlor on summer afternoons—growing ever more beautiful on the inside even as the youth and beauty faded from her face. As she once said:

> *Sex appeal in movies—especially because of those close-ups—is based purely on the surface aspects. When the bloom is off the rose, and the camera can't hide the encroaching years, you've got to have that something else, or you're all washed up ... That's the only true kind of sex appeal—when men find you fascinating and desirable even though your youth is gone ... I'm no different from any other woman in that respect—I don't like the idea of growing older.*[65]

I wish Maril had understood her true worth. Her hair, eyes, lips, and body—that was surface beauty, that was an image, that was a role she played called "Marilyn Monroe." The *real* Maril had an inner beauty, a sweetness, a shyness, and a tender heart toward children and animals that went so much deeper than mere sex appeal and being desirable to men.

Maril was a paradox; one of the strongest people I've ever known and also one of the most fragile. She was afflicted with a stage fright so intense it caused her to vomit and break out in a rash before performances. Yet she was so strong and courageous that she willed herself to stand before the cameras and deliver musical, comedic, and dramatic performances that were sheer magic. It's a tragedy she didn't understand how truly strong she was and how much character it took to achieve what she did.

She endured so much hurt and rejection that she didn't realize how much she was loved. Not just lusted after and applauded by the public, but truly *loved* by the family that adopted her—the Kargers. The rejection of her absent biological father and the abandonment of her mentally ill mother were emotional wounds from which she never recovered. I don't think she fully knew how much she meant to Nana, Daddy, Aunt Mary, Mom, my cousins, and me—the only family she had from the time she was an unknown contract player until the night she died.

At heart, in my love for her, I'm still the little girl she used to pick up from school; the girl she nicknamed "T.K." After all these years, I continue to miss Maril, not Marilyn Monroe.

Daddy grieved Maril's death very deeply. It haunted him that she passed away so young, so suddenly, so mysteriously, leaving so many unanswered questions. Aware of Maril's entanglements with the Kennedy brothers, he wondered if there was a causal connection.

Daddy and Maril never married, but they were connected heart to heart, soul to soul. And, even after their romance ended, he always cared for her and tried to help her in any way he could. It was a connection that even Maril's death couldn't sever. He continued to think about her until his own passing.

The one constant in Maril's adult life was our family, especially Nana.

Whether Maril was in Hollywood or in New York, whether she was marrying or divorcing, from that special day in early March 1948 when Daddy first brought her home to meet us, Maril had a mother to talk to and a family to come home to. I wish she had been with Nana and the rest of us on the night of August 4, 1962.

While the world lusted after Marilyn Monroe the sex goddess, our family loved Maril the sweet girl behind the goddess mask. It was Maril we knew, and it's Maril I still miss.

Having known her intimately, when I see her on-screen I remember her pre-fame days and think to myself, "Anybody can become anything in the world. You just have to keep dreaming and trying."

Maril tried so hard at everything she attempted to do. And she made it by pushing until she succeeded. Nothing was going to stop her, and nothing did. She became one of the most famous women in the world, then and now.

I have a Marilyn Monroe oil painting on black velvet created by my cousin Rita Warren; it bears a stunning likeness to a September 1953 photograph of Maril by Milton H. Greene. The painting was first given to Nana, who passed it on to my mother Patti, and now I have it.

Rita Warren's portrait of a September 1953 Marilyn Monroe photograph by Milton H. Greene (From the collection of Terry Karger)

"I just adore it," Maril once told Rita. "It really does look like me."

I think about Maril quite often. Sometimes I dream about her. The feeling of losing her when we did has never escaped me. I once dreamt Maril had a daughter of her own. Watching her hold that imaginary child, I could see her gently rocking the baby to sleep. Children were her greatest joy.

Closing my eyes, I'm six years old again, kneeling beside my little castle made of mud, hearing Daddy's car stopping in the driveway behind me. Turning to watch the car door opening, I see the foot and ankle of a lady emerging—my first glimpse of her.

Mud drips from my hands as I look into the face of an angel.

"That's a pretty house," she says.

"It's not a house. It's a castle."

"A pretty castle, then."

I hear her girlish giggle.

And I wish Maril's life had taken a different path than her premature death, that she were here with me now, and we could look back over her long life, with children of her own, continuing to laugh about good times past, reveling in simple memories.

If only …

INTERVIEWS

A̲ɴʏ ǫᴜᴏᴛᴀᴛɪᴏɴs ɴᴏᴛ ᴄɪᴛᴇᴅ in the endnotes are from interviews conducted by Jay Margolis. The interviewees included:

Ben D'Aubery
Jill D'Aubery
Caroline Barris
George Barris
Darrill Batté
Cherrill Consoli
Frank Dalton
Toni Dwiggins
Murray Garrett
Walt Lewis
Richard Meryman
Robert Miller

Don Murray
Joe Petix
Michael Reagan
Gretchen Ann Reid
Gloria Romanoff
Jane Russell
Mike Russell
Margaret Sacks
Len Steckler
Russ Tamblyn
Jacqui Warren
Johnny Warren

ENDNOTES

1   Donald Spoto, *Marilyn Monroe: The Biography* (New York: HarperCollins, 1993), 142–143.

2   Ibid., 142–143.

3   Leo Guild, "Why Marilyn Monroe Can't Cool Off!" *National Police Gazette*, January 1959, 4.

4   Marilyn Monroe, "I am a Modern Cinderella," *True Experiences*, May 1950, 22, 58–60, 62.

5   Bob Willett, " 'You've Got Me Wrong!'—Marilyn Monroe," *New Liberty*, March 1953, 58.

6   Marilyn Monroe, *My Story* (New York: Cooper Square Press, 2000), 74.

7   Ibid., 76.

8   Ibid., 75.

9   George Carpozi Jr., *The Agony of Marilyn Monroe* (London: C. Nicholls & Company, Ltd., 1962), 41–42.

10 William J. Weatherby, *Conversations with Marilyn* (New York: Mason/Charter, 1976), 147.

11 Maureen Miller, "The Private Life of Marilyn Monroe," *Screen Stars*, May 1955.

12 Monroe, *My Story*, 76.

13 Fred Lawrence Guiles, *Legend: The Life and Death of Marilyn Monroe* (New York: Stein and Day, 1984), 127.

14 Monroe, *My Story*, 78.

15 Ibid., 80–83.

16 Guiles, *Legend*, 129.
17 Natasha Lytess, as told to Jane Wilkie before Natasha's death in 1964, "My Years with Marilyn," in the collection of the Harry Ransom Humanities Research Center, the University of Texas at Austin, 4.
18 Thomas Dove, "Marilyn Monroe Tells What She Really Wants In a Man," *National Police Gazette*, October 1962, 3.
19 Lou Gerard, "MM Says: 'I Don't Like Growing Old,'" *National Enquirer*, January 11–17, 1959, 3–4.
20 Monroe, *My Story*, 16.
21 Willett, "You've Got Me Wrong," 58–59.
22 George Barris, *Marilyn: Her Life in Her Own Words* (New York: Birch Lane Press, 1995), 13.
23 Aline Mosby, "Nude Calendar Beauty at Last is Identified," *Pittsburgh (Pa.) Press*, March 13, 1952, 26.
24 John Wilcock, "Marilyn Monroe: I'm No Has-Been!" *Liberty*, July 1955, 69.
25 Ibid., 69.
26 Jane Wilkie, "He Ran Away With Her Heart," *Modern Screen*, February 1953, 35, 93–94.
27 Harrison Carroll, "Hollywood," *Evening Independent*, November 14, 1952, 4.
28 Sidney Skolsky, *Don't Get Me Wrong—I Love Hollywood* (New York: G. P. Putnam's Sons, 1975), 223.
29 Louella Parsons, "Louella Parsons' Good News," *Modern Screen*, May 1953, 8.
30 M. S. Greenman, "The Man Who Made Marilyn Sing," *Bold: The Pocket Magazine for Men*, January 1954, 15.
31 *Marilyn Monroe: Beyond the Legend* (1986), directed by Gene Feldman (Wombat Productions). The Robert Mitchum quotes are from this documentary.
32 Editors, "Exit Lines, Laughing and Otherwise," *Life*, September 27, 1954, 17.

33 Michael Sheridan, "Marilyn Doesn't Believe in Hiding Things," *Screenland*, August 1952, 55–56.

34 Guild, "Why Marilyn Monroe Can't Cool Off!," 3–4.

35 Fred Harris, "Now Marilyn Can Talk!" *Screen*, November 1956.

36 Hedda Hopper, "Marilyn Tells the Truth to Hedda Hopper," *Photoplay*, January 1953.

37 Fred Lawrence Guiles, *Norma Jeane: The Life of Marilyn Monroe* (New York: McGraw-Hill, 1969), 221.

38 Stephen Farber, "Miller & Son," *New York Times Magazine*, November 17, 1996.

39 Don McCance and the United States Submarine Veterans, *United States Submarine Veterans Inc: The First 40 Years* (Nashville: Turner Publishing, 2006), 90: LCDR Sheldon Loveless of the USS *Redfish* stated, "I knew the story of the submarine that had settled on the bottom of Tokyo Bay to elude the Japanese during WWII."

40 Carpozi Jr., *The Agony of Marilyn Monroe*, 153.

41 Guiles, *Legend*, 173–174.

42 Spoto, *Marilyn Monroe: The Biography*, 408.

43 Guiles, *Legend*, 174, 405.

44 Julian Scheer, "Carl Sandburg Talks About Marilyn Monroe," *Cavalier*, January 1963, 12–15; Editors, "Tribute to Marilyn, From a Friend … Carl Sandburg," *Look*, September 11, 1962, 90–94.

45 Barris, *Marilyn: Her Life in Her Own Words*, 126.

46 Richard Meryman, "Marilyn Monroe Lets Her Hair Down About Being Famous," *Life*, August 3, 1962, 31–34, 36, 38.

47 Ronald Kessler, *The Sins of the Father* (New York: Warner Books, 1996), 23.

48 Mona Rae Miracle, "Marilyn," *Sotheby's Auction Catalogue for the Personal Property of Marilyn Monroe: The Berniece and Mona Miracle Collection*, February 8–March 1, 2001; Sydney Roberts, "It Wasn't Suicide," *Closer*, November 3, 2014, 29–30.

49 Morris Engelberg and Marv Schneider, *DiMaggio: Setting the Record Straight* (Minnesota: MVP Books, 2004), 239.

50 Thomas T. Noguchi, M.D., and Joseph DiMona. *Coroner to the Stars*. (London: Corgi Books, 1984), 80–81.

51 Typed transcript from the estate of Hal Jacques, now in the collection of Jay Margolis.

52 Jay Margolis and Richard Buskin, *The Murder of Marilyn Monroe: Case Closed*, (New York: Skyhorse Publishing, 2016), 17–18.

53 Dr. Sidney B. Weinberg interview with George Carpozi Jr., now in the collection of Jay Margolis.

54 "Report: Man Saw Monroe Murdered," *Philadelphia Daily News*, November 18, 1982.

55 *The Marilyn Monroe Files*, live television special documentary, 1992.

56 Margolis and Buskin, *The Murder of Marilyn Monroe*, 49–61, 281.

57 Ibid., 28–30, 50, 267–268.

58 Anthony Summers, *Goddess: The Secret Lives of Marilyn Monroe*, (London: Phoenix, 2000), 537.

59 Ibid., 391–392, 538.

60 Margolis and Buskin, *The Murder of Marilyn Monroe*, 1–27, 60, 201–214, 331.

61 James A. Hudson. *The Mysterious Death of Marilyn Monroe: Suicide?, Accidental?, Murder?* (New York: Volitant, 1968), 98; *History's Mysteries: The Death of Marilyn Monroe*, Documentary, A&E Television Networks, 2000.

62 Margolis and Buskin, *The Murder of Marilyn Monroe*, 28.

63 Rock Positano and John Positano, *Dinner with DiMaggio: Memories of An American Hero* (New York: Simon & Schuster, 2017), 178.

64 Mary Ellen Snodgrass, *Encyclopedia of Feminist Literature* (New York: Facts on File, 2006), 272.

65 Gerard, "MM Says: 'I Don't Like Growing Old,'" 3–4.